AWESOME TRUTH THAT MAKES SENSE

THE PUBLISHER

BAC (Bill & Ann Carraway) Publications was born 11-01-92 from a desire, a dream, and a determination.

Awesome Truth That Makes Sense is BAC's fifth publication–three for clients, two by Bill.

Why tackle the multifaceted behemoth of book publishing? This question reminds me of the man who was asked, "Why do you climb mountains?" His answer was, "Because they're there." Writing/publishing is there, and I want to be a part of it

During the 45 years I was pastor of 14 churches, I often dreamed of this pursuit in retirement. I couldn't do it then, because for me pastoring was a full-time job. So is writing/publishing.

When I began my new venture, I did not even know what P.C. meant. I now own my second one! Learning computing is not easy, but too, it's not impossible. The same can be said for putting an article, or even a book together. As a church hymn vows, "I'll bear the toil, endure the pain, Supported by thy Word," one in my shoes endures because he is determined.

Thank you, God bless you, Gordon Peterson for the opportunity to work for and with you on this, your production. Many more messages like this one are needed. It is my prayer that **you** will write them, and allow BAC Publications to produce them.

WB (Bill) Carraway
(972) 491-9318

Awesome Truth That Makes Sense

IT'S TIME FOR CLEAR THINKING

GORDON Wm. PETERSON

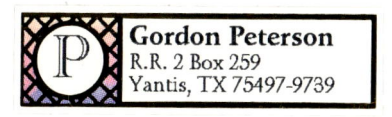

P **Gordon Peterson**
R.R. 2 Box 259
Yantis, TX 75497-9739

BAC PUBLICATIONS
P. O. Box 224371
Dallas, Texas 75222

Copyright © by Gordon Wm. Peterson

All Rights Reserved

Biblical Quotations

All Bible quotations in this book are taken from the New International Version unless otherwise indicated.

Library of Congress
Catalogue Card Number
98-74277

International Standard Book Number
0-9633855-4-2

Published by
BAC Publications
Dallas, Texas 75222

Printed in the
United States of America

CONTENTS

Epigram 7
Foreword 9
Preface 11 - 12

One   A Sure Bet   13 - 33

Two   Evolution Disproved   35 - 42

Three   Healing Miracles   43 - 56

Four   Theory Versus Fact   57 - 95

Five   Working Truth   97 - 119

Six   New Life Tools   121 - 133

Seven   Prayer's Power   135 - 164

Eight   Salvation's Plan   165 - 194

Nine   It's Action Time   195 - 203

Ten   We Can Do It   205 - 219

Bibliography - 221 - 224
Index - 225 - 228

JESUS SAID:

"And ye shall know the truth, and the truth shall make you free" (John 8:32 KJV).

FOREWORD

What a terrific book!. I think it will be especially helpful to anyone in Christian service. Both laymen and ministers will find it very useful. Gordon Peterson is a real man of God and has put his best thoughts forward in this fine book.

Bill Glass
Founder & CEO
Weekend of Champions
Nationwide Prison Ministry

PREFACE

This book is written to proclaim the sureness of the truth of God, the Bible, creation, Jesus Christ as our only promised Messiah, the Holy Spirit, prayer, soul, heaven, hell and Satan and his evil spirits. My intention is to bring to light the hidden details that are normally taken lightly and given little thought to, so readers can realize the awesomeness of God's realm.

Being a machinist by trade, I esteem machining because in that craft a technique usually is either right or wrong with no tolerance for any in-between. There is no matter of opinion, as in most other vocations. In machining, facts must not be distorted or ignored. If every designed detail is not obeyed, a very expensive machined part can be rendered worthless. This point is essential to what I am about to say in the following paragraph concerning my attitude in discussing this book's contents.

I do not wish in any way to distort, change, or minimize any part of the Bible, or other documented evidence to explain or prove the certainty of God in His universe. All questions to God's work in this world should be settled by documented truth, rather than unproved theories.

I respectfully credit you with as much integrity as I claim for myself. Therefore, I will deal with facts that make sense to the open-minded individual, but I will also document my sources and give additional available references in the bibliography rather than in the text. I do this because my purpose in this book is to communicate, not to sound intellectual in my own right.

PREFACE [Continued from previous page]

I hope this book will stimulate thought and give answer to important questions. My wish is that not only my words within the book will be read, but also the added resource materials. I do not expect anyone to accept unproved theories from me or anyone else. Much to the contrary, I advocate staying with truth that makes sense and with sources that are reliable.

Gordon Wm. Peterson

CHAPTER ONE
A SURE BET

Are you climbing the wrong mountain? Are you looking for pie in the sky or a million dollars to fall into your lap? The obsession of our society is to get something for nothing. Most of us have a desire to win something, to be given lots of money for no effort, or to hold the winning ticket–a five-dollar investment with a one-in-a-million chance to win.

Even the weather forecasts are on a percentage basis, as are political elections. Candidate A is a 55-to-45 favorite over Opponent B, which in itself isn't bad, but many go for easy money by betting on the odds.

Since most voting is based on popularity, rather than qualification, election results are not predictable. In sports, especially at playoff time, odds might favor A over B, either to win or to do so by a certain score. Here again, people are betting on something that isn't for sure. Ardent research is conducted on both teams to come up with a sure-fire answer, but during the game, if the favorite fumbles the ball a couple of times, the sure bet is lost.

In middleman betting, as in horse racing, the odds may be even or 1 to 40 (which pays $40 for a $1 bet). This sounds good, but the nag may be so slow, there's probably less than a 1-to-40 chance he will win. Consider also that the track organization takes out a profit of up to 30 percent of the winnings, the license tax is probably 20 percent of each dollar, and the horse owners take part of the winnings. So the winner's pot has shrunk considerably. All of this says that the odds are against you before you start. The real winner is the race track. So betting on a horse race is a long shot from a sure thing.

What about the state lottery? Of course this is a way of the state taxing you, and the winnings are to entice you to pay. But the lottery company takes out much that the government never sees, besides cutting your odds even more.

Casinos operate with about the same efficiency. In this operation one does not buy tickets, but can put money on the "sure thing" all night and still keep on losing. We recall the well-known story of the man who drove to Las Vegas in a Mercedes Benz and with $50,000 but returned home on a $200,000 Greyhound bus and broke. Quite the opposite of a sure thing.

The familiar sweepstakes sometime have odds of one to 10 million or more of winning the Grand Prize of up to

$10 million dollars, which the sponsor takes 20 to 30 years to pay. This is less than 5 percent of the original per year. So the sponsoring organization still has the million dollars, or even more if it is rightly invested. This is definitely not a sure thing, yet many hopefully try for it.

These pastime pursuits along with cockfights, dog racing, raffles, bingo, dice and many other games of chance are unsure ways to easy money. All of these gambles make someone else rich, but when we do have that one-in-a-million win, it's usually "easy come; easy go," making one's windfall short-lived or leaving a snare that divides families. At other times the winnings will go for dope and drinking, thereby bringing a curse of addiction. In other words, *it ain't what it's cracked up to be!*

It's been said, truthfully I think, that most humans can handle poverty but few can cope with money. Even if we do by chance come into a lot of money, still that is not a guarantee of good living, health, happiness and security.

Also there are those who patronize fortunetellers, palm readers, and give credence to crystal balls, astrology and psychics, witchcraft, the occult, and Ouija boards. All such are wild guesses, usually for the purpose of making money off of people. Watch out! These lures are addictive and seductive, and if they should work at all, it would be by the power of Satan. In this world of chance, there is something that's proven to be sure and worthy of our acceptance—even that which we can stake

CHAPTER ONE

our lives on. If we, to be honest, will go to the very root of proof, there is a sure evidence awaiting us. And of that, we can be sure.

For one of the many sure bets in life, let's begin with Moses and the Israelites as they spent 40 years in the desert crossing to the Promised Land. This journey can easily be checked out in the *National Geographic,* December, 1948 article, "Sinai Sheds New Light on the Bible." The article tells of the findings and experiences of archaeologists on a desert expedition. They followed the route of the Israelites by the pottery dropped in the sand by the former captives who departed from Egypt to a land flowing with milk and honey, which was to be their permanent home. Two U.S. Army surplus six-by-six trucks, loaded with ample supplies, augmented the expedition, which is quite a contrast to Moses' trip.

The archaeologists were startled by the loneliness of the wilderness, with scarcely a living plant or animal in the vast expanse of sand. They labeled the region "One of the most desolate places on earth."

The expedition traveled hour after hour over the desert territory, filled with nothing. Then suddenly, the horror of lifelessness was broken by a little gray and brown bird, with blue under its wings, flying from one rock to another. It probably meant that they were nearing the Gulf of Suez. The group could easily imagine the discouragement of the Israelites, as reported in Exodus 17:3: "But the people were thirsty for water there, and they grumbled against Moses. They said `Why did you bring us up out of Egypt to make us and our children

A SURE BET PAGE 17

and livestock die of thirst?'" *Time Magazine*, March 23, 1981 also had an article concerning the route of Moses and the Israelite path, so it can be confirmed and not argued away. The Exodus is the gospel truth. It really happened. But now we examine some facts that are not detailed in the Biblical account.

We all know, when we stop to consider it, that a person or animal alone in the hot desert would last only a few days without cloud cover or would, on some nights, freeze without the cover. Yet the Israelites lived 40 years there so there had to have been a cloud covering for the entire 40 years, as recorded in Exodus 13:21-22: "By day the Lord went ahead of them in a pillar of cloud to guide them on their way and by night in a pillar of fire to give them light, so that they could travel by day or night. Neither the pillar of cloud by day nor the pillar of fire by night left its place in front of the people."

Now for the sure odds. There is 1 chance in a hundred that one would even see a cloud in the desert sky or, to say it another way, to see 1 cloud every hundred hours. The chances, on any given hour, for a cloud to be large enough to cover the entire camp of some 2 million people for an entire hour would be somewhere close to 1 chance in a thousand. But the cloud cover existed, not just for 1 hour or each hour for 10 hours or 24 hours or a week, month, year but each hour for 40 years. An analyst would say that the odds diminish by the power of 10 with each step; the more the hours, the less the chance. It would be like one chance in a thousand for the cloud to appear for 1 hour, but maybe 1 chance in

10 thousand that it would happen 2 hours in a row. Or did God have a hand in it all? Surely, it couldn't have happened by sheer chance. I'm betting (believing) God was in full control.

The 2 million figure is based on Exodus 12:37 which states that the number of Israelites was 600 thousand men. Add the women, children, and non Israelites who were in the departing number, and the 2 million figure is plausible. No telling what their number was 40 years later when they were ready to invade Canaan. Regardless of the exact number, there were a lot of mouths to feed, especially in a land where there is hardly enough food to feed a sparrow. If each person ate one pound of food a day and a conservative figure of even 1 million people is taken, that would be 1 million pounds per day or 500 tons or 10 railroad boxcars full of food per day. This is not just for 1 day or 1 week or 1 month or 1 year, but each and every day for 40 years. This provision had to be a miracle of God. The food definitely had to be manna from heaven.

An army officer who calculated the amount of food needed, using 3.5 million people [and in time, Israel grew to that number] and 2 or 3 pounds of food each day per person, arrived at a figure of more than 100 boxcars full of food for a daily requirement. He's probably right, but that much is not required to make the event totally impossible to achieve without God's miraculous power. But I stay with a more conservative number of 1 million. The Bible states that God provided a special food (manna) for His wandering children. Exodus 16:16: "This is what the Lord has commanded:

Each one is to gather as much as he needs. Take an omer for each person you have in your tent.'"[An omer is about 3 quarts in English measure]

One scientist tried to explain the miracle away by saying a moss forms sometimes in the desert, which the Israelites most likely lived on. From what I understand, there wouldn't be enough of this to form naturally in 30 days on 100 acres to feed 1 person, even if it were palatable.

Numbers 11:6,7,9 explains, "But we have lost our appetite; we never see anything but this manna. The manna was like coriander seed and looked like resin. When the dew settled on the camp at night, the manna also came down."

How does one calculate odds when the impossible happens? Manna, in great abundance, is all over the ground where ordinarily there isn't enough food for 1 person, much less several million. Manna is the grand prize (highest award), an omer for each and all of the millions of people each and every morning for 40 years. And obviously it was a food with all the nutrients the body needed. It kept the wanderers healthy the entire time so that they were fruitful and multiplied. Also there was a second miracle. Throughout the 40 years in the desert, neither their clothes nor their shoes wore out (Deuteronomy 29:5).

Re: their health, wouldn't a health food company pay a handsome price for the manna formula! That company could make millions of dollars. It was a most loving and generous gift of a free grocery bill for all the millions of winners for 40 years. Everyone, who trusted, obeyed and followed God was a winner. There was not one loser. This had to be and surely was a miracle from God Himself. "The Israelites ate manna 40 years, until they came to a land that was settled; they ate manna until they reached the border of Canaan." (Exodus 16:35) All this happened where there was no vegetation. Nothing alive. No natural odds, no normal odds. Nothing! And when the crowd (on a mission for Jehovah) griped about the manna, God caused quail to fly into the camp, and the Israelites ate their full, until they were sick (Numbers 11:4-34). Using logic, we know the food had to come from somewhere. The Israelites had to eat because they certainly couldn't fast that long. The Biblical account of manna from heaven has to be true. Like it or not, we must accept this miracle of God. We cannot explain it away or cast doubt on it. It has to be a gift of God's love.

With this background, Jesus' feeding the 5 thousand and the 4 thousand isn't hard to believe. Neither is the virgin birth of Christ. These events were our miracle-working God in action again. Nothing's too hard for Him.

The discovery of the Dead Sea Scrolls in a cave at Qumran, at the north end of the Dead Sea in Palestine, adds to our proof. The Scroll I, which contains at least part of the gospel of Mark, was found in cave # 7. Mark 6:52,53, which was buried A.D. 68, refers to the feeding of the 5 thousand. So the Bible was written and distributed within 35 years of the events having happened.

(Please refer to Grant Jeffery's book, *Signature of God*, Page 103 for confirmation.) The scroll is yet another proof of the sureness of truth found in the Bible, the Word of God.

In our investigation, let's not forget the desert's most vital and precious need. The Israelites had to have water to drink where there is no water. What about an oasis? One, generally, would not have lasted 1 full hour if each person used 1 gallon of water per day, using the conservative figure of 1 million people. And this does not count the water necessary for the livestock. Therefore, the amount of water needed would be the equivalent of a lake 200 feet long by 140 feet wide by 5 feet deep each and every day. I doubt any oasis contains that amount of water.

So again, if we are going to use honest and true logic, we must go with the Biblical account of Moses striking the rock to produce water or throwing a tree into the water to make the bitter water sweet. "Arriving at Marah, they couldn't drink the water because it was bitter (that is why the place was called Marah, meaning bitter). Then the people turned against Moses. `Must we die of thirst?' they demanded. Moses pleaded with the Lord to help them, and the Lord showed him a tree to throw into the water, and the water became sweet." (Exodus 15:23-25, LBT) Emphasizing the necessity of water, the Israelites became very impatient until God's command was obeyed by Moses and the water became drinkable. Again, a total miracle by our awesome God. Concerning chances to win, every day all Israel were winners, receiving the jackpot of life-giving water, i.e., water in the desert where there was no chance of winning (getting water), except for God's provision. God has promised always to provide His children's needs, but not necessarily their wants.

Never forget that in reaching the desert, the Israelites had a gigantic barrier to cross–the Red Sea. Skeptics try to nullify this miracle by contending that the crossing place was a marsh and also by saying that the crossing was in a place different from the Biblical record. Their crossing quickly was essential because the Egyptian army was on their heels, bent on slaughter. But our awesome God turned the tables on the enemy and the Egyptians were the ones slaughtered. This miracle is recorded in Exodus 14:9-31 and is certainly the only logical way Israel could have escaped from Egypt. God did, as He always does, everything He had to do to preserve a lineage through which the Savior of the world was to be born. God did it out of His awesome love for the whole world, as did Jesus in His willingness to suffer unto death on the cross for our sins. Truly, "Jesus paid it all."

Yet there's still another river to cross–for the Israelites. When God's chosen people reached the Jordan River, 40 years later, Joshua had replaced Moses, who had died. Since God's power had now shifted to Joshua, the waters of the Jordan parted, just as did the Red Sea for Moses. The Israelites again crossed over on dry land. Joshua 3:15-17 records the event: "Now the Jordan is at flood stage all during harvest. Yet as soon as the priests who carried the ark reached the Jordan and their feet touched the water's edge, the water from upstream stopped flowing. It piled up in a heap a great distance away, at a town called Adam in the vicinity of Zarethan, while the water flowing down to the Sea of the Arabah (the Salt Sea) was completely cut off. So the people crossed over opposite Jericho. The priests who carried the ark of the covenant of the Lord stood firm on dry ground in the middle of the Jordan, while all Israel passed by until the whole nation had completed the crossing on dry ground."

This parting of the waters wouldn't happen naturally in a trillion years, yet it did happen at an opportune time of tremendous need. The chosen people had to cross the river, and God provided the way. Surely we serve an awesome, powerful, and loving God.

Psychics and seers of today make prophecies at the beginning of each year about things sure to happen that year, even one of which seldom occurs. Yet these charlatans are sought out at a price by a gullible public.

But in contrast, we now look at the most awesome and proven fulfillment of all prophecies. From 400 to 1400 years in advance, scholars agree that more than 300 prophecies were made that were to be fulfilled in one person designated the Messiah. All of these prophecies were fulfilled in the birth, life, and death of Jesus Christ.

A former pastor of mine told often of a firm that set aside $1 million to be given to anyone who could find one prophecy unfulfilled in the earthly ministry of Jesus Christ. No one ever collected that prize. I never heard

PAGE 24 CHAPTER ONE

this statement from any other source, but I believe it to be true. A Westmont college professor says that for just eight of these prophecies to be fulfilled in one person is equal to covering Texas two feet deep with silver dollars and marking one. Then mixing them thoroughly and having a blind man walk around for days; then stop, dig down, and pick out the marked coin on the first try.

In reference to the Westmont professor's statement, I believe there are more than eight prophecies concerning Christ recorded. At the time of Christ there were some 15 historians who wrote about Him and Christianity.[1] But there were over 300 prophecies, all fulfilled in the coming of Jesus Christ. This is far beyond our comprehension. Over 300 chances and every one a winner, that is, a sure bet.

Another analogist says that for 48 prophecies to be fulfilled in one person is impossible but again there were over 300 which is six times impossible. To me that is more reasonable than the fact I'm writing this and that you are reading it.

One of these prophecies that prominently stands out is the famous 70 weeks of years, made some 483 years earlier in Daniel 9:24: "Seventy 'sevens' are decreed for your people and your holy city to finish transgressions, to put an end to sin, to atone for wickedness, to bring everlasting righteousness, to seal up vision and prophecy and to anoint the most holy." Is this foretelling credible and has it come to pass? Read on and you will see.

1. *Why I Believe*, by Dr. D. James Kennedy, Page 96

This prophecy comes out to A.D. 26, exactly the year of Christ's anointing. This alone is a one-in-a-million chance. [2]

Another interesting prophecy is found in Micah 5:2: "But you, Bethlehem, Ephrathah, though you are small among the clans of Judah, out of you will come for me one who will be ruler over Israel, whose origins are from of old, from ancient times."

This Bethlehem was not a town at the time Micah prophesied. Ephrathah was the county the new Bethlehem was in, not the other old Bethlehem of Zebulon in the north. This prophecy was made 700 years before its fulfillment. Again the odds are next to impossible that it would come to pass but the prophecy was right on target.

Some 26 other religious leaders have no prophecy whatsoever about them, only Christ. Since His coming was obviously foretold by God, we do well to heed the warning Christ gave us: "For false Christs and false prophets will appear and perform signs and miracles to deceived the elect–if that were possible" (Mark 13:22),

The Bible is all about Jesus, both in the Old and New Testaments. It is also the only book of any religion full of prophecies and their fulfillment. Of the nearly 2 thousand prophecies in the Old Testament, all are fulfilled in the same Old Testament, plus the 300 prophecies regarding Christ's first coming. The Bible is the only religious book based on godly and heavenly facts.

2. Dr. D. James Kennedy, Video Tape, January, 1995.

Archaeologists keep confirming this claim more and more in their digs. (Check out this claim in *Signature Of God* by Grant Jeffery.) God has left us sure proof of the veracity of His Word.

Even some prophecies on the second coming of Christ are already fulfilled. Of the 257 prophecies relating to Christ's second coming, according to scholars, most have been fulfilled and more are being fulfilled almost daily. The time is very near; Christ could burst through the sky at any moment. So what time is it? It's time to be ready, to be looking up, and not to be caught napping and unprepared. Jesus warned of false Christs rising up in the last days before His return: "For false Christs and false prophets will appear and perform great signs and miracles to deceive even the elect–if that were possible" (Matthew 24:24). Therefore, we should be on guard against being deceived. Satan (an angel of light) is working overtime.

Jesus gives 2 other warnings against false Christs in the same chapter as He said in Matthew 24:5 and Matthew 24:11: "For many will come in my name, claiming 'I am the Christ,' and will deceive many." And "and many false prophets will appear and deceive many people."

The warning is sounded again in Mark 13:5-6: "Jesus said to them: Watch out that no one deceives you. Many will come in my name, claiming, 'I am he,' and will deceive many." We've seen at least some fulfillment of this warning already in bold and deceitful ones claiming majestical power, but they are fakes and in time are proved so. Their disciples show no life-changing effect.

This kind of preaching is propagated by Satan and should be shunned vehemently and continuously each time it occurs.

A second coming prophecy that is being fulfilled now is made by Jesus in Matthew 24:7-10: "Nation will rise against nation, and kingdom against kingdom. There will be famines and earthquakes in various places. Then you will be handed over to be persecuted and put to death, and you will be hated by all nations because of me. At that time many will turn away from the faith and will betray and hate each other,"

Focusing on earthquakes alone, the *World Almanac, 1994,* reported 75 from A.D. 526 to 1980, and 26 from February 13, 1992 to August 8, 1993. A third as many occurred in less than one and one-half years as did in 1,454 years. Definitely, this fact is a distinct fulfillment of the earthquake prophecy in these last days.

And what about pestilence? AIDS is perhaps the worst epidemic ever to hit society, and following on its heels in severity is cancer. Numerous other diseases that have become immune to the latest drugs lurk in the shadows. Another menace to many continents is drought, killing people by the thousands, especially in Africa.

An additional horror in our world is Christianity's being unlawful in many countries, even carrying the death penalty. However, I hear that this severity has lessened somewhat temporarily, fulfilling another prophecy in Matthew 24:14: "And this gospel of the kingdom will be preached in the whole world as a testimony to all nations, and then the end will come." Today television and radio blanket the earth with the use of satellite stations orbiting the sky. The Billy Graham Evangelistic Association has held two worldwide crusades, reaching almost every country in the world at one time through television and radio. Almost everyone could have either seen or heard the American evangelist by putting forth the effort.

Then there's the Trinity Broadcasting Network on television, and there are radio stations in most countries of the world broadcasting the Word of God daily. The Internet, with close to worldwide coverage, is proclaiming God's Word effectively, and the devil has been–so far–unable to stop the spread.

Wycliffe Bible Translators (WBT) are translating God's holy Word (the Bible) into every written or unwritten language, even where the starting point is to make or print an alphabet and a dictionary. More than 450 New Testament translations have been completed, but 3,000 languages yet remain to be put into the heart language of the respective people. WBT is also assisting other missions in Biblical translation in an effort to allow every people group in the world the privilege of having God's Word in their native heart language. Furthermore, many nations are establishing their own Bible translating organizations. Also efforts are now underway to program computers to do the complete translation.

Campus Crusade for Christ, founded by Bill Bright, is covering almost every country of the world with the *Jesus Film*, which is effectively spreading the good news of the gospel. Bright's *Four Spiritual Laws,* with over 2.5 billion copies printed with worldwide distribution, is another strong tool for getting people into the Word.

Dr. D. James Kennedy with *Evangelism Explosion* is working in almost every country of the world training soul winners. *Every Home for Christ Mission* (EHC) has set a goal of visiting every home in the world with the gospel message by the year A.D. 2000. The American Bible Society and World Home Bible League (and many others) are printing Bibles by the millions translated into most languages of the world, a work that is creating great spiritual demand. The Bill Glass Ministries are working in prisons, citywide crusades, and a youth program to bring people to Christ. Let us pray that more Bible-printing organizations will be born. All of these endeavors are borne along by stalwarts of sterling character.

How encouraging are the thousands of missions and ministries God is using to fill in the gaps of world missions during these last days to reach everyone with the saving knowledge of Christ's gospel. Jesus' prophecy that the gospel will be preached all over the world is steadily being realized. Beyond a shadow of a doubt, God is in complete control, doing a most important work that cannot be ignored.

The "mark of the beast," mentioned in Revelation 13:16-18 as the sign of loyalty to the "beast" and a necessity for buying or selling activities, seemed impossible just a few years ago, but the recent computer chip has changed that. This new discovery, the size of a fingernail, can be inserted under the skin of the forehead or hand, carrying thousands of informational bits pertaining to a person. Predictions are that it will replace credit card and cash usage in a noncash society. Reportedly, it is already being used on a trial basis in some areas of the world on people and pet animals.

What more do we need for a sure proof of God's Biblical authority? The mark of the beast is a 2,000 year-old prophecy and more current than today's newspaper.Let us–in humility and faith–stake our very lives on the veracity of God's Word. Prophecies such as these amaze the human mind, but in reality they are merely the workings of Almighty God. For all who reply, "But I don't understand," consider this. If God were small enough for mere humans to understand Him, He would not be big enough to handle everything in the universe and love us like He does. He is an awesome God, and His Word must not be compromised.

Another 1900-year-old prophecy being fulfilled today is Revelation 1:7: "Look, he is coming with the clouds, and every eye will see him, even those who pierced him; and all the peoples of the earth will mourn because of him. So shall it be! Amen." Before television and the satellite stations, this prophecy seemed absurd. It is also true that when the prophecy was made, some 30 years after Christ's death, those of that day had no idea how it could happen, but God knew that the necessary vehicles to carry out the prophecy would come. Now it is easily understood how Christ may be visible to people all over the world in all His super power and glory upon His return to earth. Remember that twice God prophesied He would bring His people into the Promised Land, which He did. "Take some of the first fruits of all that you produce from the soil of the land the Lord your God is giving you and put them in a basket. Then go to the place the Lord your God will choose for a dwelling for his Name and say to the priest in office at the time, 'I declare today to the Lord your God that I have come to the land the Lord swore to our forefathers to give us" (Deuteronomy 26:2-3). The promise was kept even after 40 years in the desert. Yes, God was faithful, but that isn't all.

Again, referring to the last times, God says, "For I will take you from among the heathen, and gather you out of all countries, and will bring you into your own land" Ezekiel 36:24, KJV). This seemed impossible in the 1930s when the land of the ancient Israelites was almost totally barren with not even a dead stick to be found for a fire, but Israel became a nation in the 1940s. Further reading in this passage reveals that God promised to make the land fruitful again, which has now happened to the extent that Europe now gets most of her produce from Israel. God is surely faithful beyond comprehension.

But still there are more of God's awesome predictions being fulfilled before our very eyes. In Nahum 2:4 we're told: "The chariots storm through the streets, rushing back and forth through the squares. They look like flaming torches; they dart about like lighting." Such a scene was unimaginable when it was predicted 2300 years ago, but it's commonplace with us. Our cars, with headlights, speed through the streets, but our airplanes travel much faster. Spacecraft go somewhat like the lightning, especially in comparison to horses of those days. Last-day prophecies are being fulfilled. Yet there is more.

"The ten horns you saw are ten kings who have not yet received a kingdom, but who for one hour will receive authority as kings along with the best. These words are recorded in Revelation 17:12 as God's angel (messenger) made them known to John the beloved apostle, exiled on the Isle of Patmos by the Roman government. Now we turn to Daniel 7:20 and read, "I also wanted to know about the ten horns on its head and about the other horn that came up, before which three of them fell-the horn that looked more imposing than the others and that had eyes and a mouth that spoke boastfully." This is the European common market and has come to pass. Quite a specific prophecy, not just a shot in the dark. The whole world is affected. It had to be made of God. It's a part of the new world order.

Much more in Bible prophecy is coming to pass today and the Apostle Paul hit it right on the head:"But mark this: There will be terrible times in the last days. People will be lovers of themselves, lovers of money, boastful, proud, abusive, disobedient to their parents, ungrateful, unholy, without love, unforgiving, slanderous, without self-control, brutal, not lovers of the good, treacherous, rash, conceited, lovers of pleasure rather than lovers of God–having a form of godliness but denying its power. Have nothing to do with them"(2 Timothy 3:1-5).Paul talked; now it's our turn. We all get uptight when God's commands and laws interfere with what we want to do. We make our belief fit our sins; yet that doesn't change a thing! Hell is still hell, heaven is still heaven. Like it or not, we mortals don't run things. God does. He makes the rules and He is in charge. Mark Twain said, "We don't reject the Bible because of its contradictions, but because it contradicts us." The redeemed are those who are sold out to Jesus. Are you?

Strong and credible belief exists that Noah's ark has been found, even with the boulders with rope eyelets in one end for anchors. Reports say that it has broken up with part of it in a crevice. Also signs abound that a great flood covered the earth at one time and the family of Noah escaped in the ark. If the Bible says it, I believe it. Creation, another mystery, is being more and more understood by scientists today.

Evolutionists are coming up with all kinds of explanations of how the earth began and humans appeared, except they leave God out of it. An illustration is the big-bang theory. But who caused the big bang?

CHAPTER TWO
EVOLUTION DISPROVED

The earth is 1 big magnet, having a north and south pole as all magnets and compasses have. This magnetism in the needed amount is essential for life to exist on our planet, according to scientists. Magnetism could not evolve but had to be created by God to the maximum strength of what the earth could tolerate. This fact is also true regarding other planets.

A Russian scientist found, by checking the magnetism of the earth daily, that it was weakening or deteriorating at a noticeable rate. His discovery made him realize scientific logic, in such circumstances, of there being a beginning or a maximum of the earth's full capacity. Consequently, he formulated a calculation of the number of years necessary to return to the maximum amount of magnetism, finding it to be 6,000 minimum to 10,000 maximum years. Desiring only the truth, the Russian scientist asked about a dozen of his associates to double-check his answer. They did, arriving at the same conclusion. Working from his confirmed formula, he was convinced that the theory of evolution could not have created the universe and its life in that short period of time, yet it was obvious to any sensible person that creation happened. Therefore, there had to be a creator. Reverting back to the Biblical account of creation, the Russian came to the firm conviction that God "created the heavens and the earth" (Genesis 1:1). But his persuasion didn't stop there. He began a serious study of the Bible, which led to his accepting Christ as his Savior and Lord, and getting right with *his* creator, God. Previously, the scientist had insisted that science agree with the evolution theory, but his honesty in "just sticking with the facts" persuaded him that it didn't, doesn't, and cannot work.

According to another major scientist, for one life cell to evolve from the elements depends on one chance in 10 to the $40,000^{th}$ power, which means it is utterly impossible. Our schools, in reality, are betting on this impossible chance, with odds of zero, in teaching evolution. Teaching evolution as fact is propagating a lie.

In the area of the Creation Evidence Museum in Glen Rose, Texas, 208 dinosaur tracks are found among 57 human tracks, plus a petrified human finger. Their being found together indicates dinosaurs and humans were on the earth at the same time. In the same stratum at Glen Rose fossils that became extinct 500 million years ago were found, along with fossils of life that became extinct 50 million years ago, according to evolutionists' dating. Fossils of plants were unearthed whose existence goes back 250 million years along with dinosaurs who lived 100 million years before that. One of the dinosaurs was 20 feet high and 40 feet long. Found also were tracks of cats that date back 6 million years. Since all of the listed were found in the same stratus, that means they all lived in the same period of time. This fact destroys the Carbon 14 Theory of testing the age of findings and destroys the evolution theory that depends heavily on carbon dating.

Clarence Darrow, in the famous Scopes Trial at Dayton, Tennessee, in July 1925, used a tooth as the missing link between ape and man. Darrow claimed that the tooth came from the partial jaw of a male body in Nebraska ("the Nebraska man"), but further excavation in 1926 unearthed the remainder of the jaw, which proved to be that of a peccary (wild pig). As a result of the 11-day trial, which should have been reversed, as the evidence was disproved, our schools have been teaching evolution as a fact since that time. Now, 73 years later, there is still no missing link, which proves, beyond the shadow of a doubt, there was no evolution, but God created the universe. Truly, He is the great God of the universe.[3]

It is impossible for any of us to create God or a god, but God created us and everything that exists. Creation is a deliberate, intellectual production, not a chance occurrence. Nature points to a purposeful designer, whose masterpiece (creation) works beautifully. How can anyone deny that God–in providing flowers, birds, fish, and quality foods–did so strictly for humankind's pleasure and benefit? Think how beneficial are the planets.

---

3. The video tape, *Creation in Symphony*, may be ordered from Creation Evidence Museum, PO Box 309, Glen Rose, Texas 76043, phone (817) 897-3200.

CHAPTER TWO

The sun gives mankind light and heat; the moon and stars give us light and guidance at night, as well as creating and regulating ocean tides; the tilt of the earth causes our seasons and even each day's length. All of this–and much more–is worked out to the tiniest detail in God's glorious plan.

Consider some other wonders of God's creation:
1. A variety of snails that actually shoots darts.
2. A Rossy fish that swims into the open mouth of predator fish and cleans their teeth. In fact, the predator fish line up in turn for this service, like men waiting in line for a barber to cut their hair. Evolution? I think not.
3. There are plants and flowers that eat insects by luring them in and closing on them, and other plants, flowers, and insects that depend on each other for survival and reproduction.
4. The giraffe's heart must pump blood through its long neck. To prevent lightheadedness when the head is up or avoid bursting blood vessels when the head is down, the giraffe is equipped with valves in the blood vessels to maintain uniform pressure at all positions.

These are just a few of the natural wonders of God's creation.

Nature, as it is labeled, in reality is God's computer, programmed by Him to do all the miraculous things, which we take for granted. Nature should not be referred to as "Mother Nature" since nature is the handiwork of God. We worship God, not His work as found in nature.

Job 40:15-24 reminds us: "Look at the behemoth, which I made along with you and which feeds on grass like an ox. What strength he has in his loins, what power in the muscles of his belly! His tail sways like a cedar, the sinews of his thighs are close-knit. His bones are tubes of bronze, his limbs like rods of iron. He ranks first among the works of God, yet his Maker can approach him with his sword. The hills bring him their produce, and all the wild animals play nearby. Under the lotus plants he lies, hidden among the reeds in the marsh. The lotuses conceal him in their shadow; the poplars by the stream surround him. When the river rages, he is not alarmed; he is secure, though the Jordan should surge against his mouth. Can anyone capture him by the eyes, or trap him and pierce his nose?"

Some translations say that the behemoth is an elephant, or a hippopotamus, but neither of these has a tail like a cedar tree. Yet the dinosaur does. The elephant isn't that much at home in the water, but the dinosaur is. The hippopotamus feeds mostly in or near the water, not generally in the hills as stated in these verses, but the dinosaur does. It's generally unsafe to be near elephants or the hippopotamus, but the dinosaurs feed on grass like the ox, which means he probably is not dangerous to all the wild animals that play nearby. To each animal existing in this passage, God says, "which I made along with you," indicating that they were made at the same time.

My feeling is that the animal referred to here is a type of dinosaur, especially now that man and dinosaur tracks are found in the Glen Rose area as having lived at the same time. The dinosaur totally fits the description. God's Word proves right again. The name "dinosaur" is only some 200 years old. The rest of the story in Job 41 pertains to the leviathan,[4] which also lived during Bible times. The description is very specific regarding the creature's size and strength, which are also mentioned in Psalm 74:14 and Isaiah 27:1.

Is Noah's flood (as it is called) really fact? The finding of Noah's ark has already been mentioned. Expeditions of the past century prove the ark's existence. One such expedition even returned with wood from the relic, but presently investigators are barred from the area. If the ark exists, and evidence is quite concrete that it does, it shows God's great love and concern in prolonging the lineage of man and the world's creatures by revealing to Noah—more than a century ahead of time—to build a boat on dry land in preparation for the flood.

The people then (as people do now) ridiculed and laughed at that promise of God. Likewise today, people scorn prophecies concerning the second coming of Christ. They spurn it with excuses such as "I don't want to be a fanatic," "It all evolved," "I'll do what I want to do," "Everybody's doing it," and some scoff that God doesn't even exist.

The real reason for their defiance is their desire to be self-propelled. "Nobody's gonna tell me how to live, not even God—if there is a God." This type of attitude leads to immoral acts of riotous living that, in turn, lead

---

[4]. Bible, possibly the crocodile. 2. any huge marine animal, as the whale.
The Random House College Dictionary Revised Edition, copyright 1998

EVOLUTION DISPROVED PAGE 41

to self-destruction. Just as God's law of gravity cannot be disobeyed without hurt or death, neither can God's moral laws. But many in the present generation pay no more attention to God's declarations and warnings than did those of Noah's day. In other words, disbelief and its resultant defiance of God run in the human family.

Most countries have historical stories of a great flood. Can they all be wrong? There really was a worldwide flood–a great water upheaval. This fact explains the many different plants and mammals, which the evolutionists date becoming extinct from 550 million to 6,000 years ago, now being found in fossil state in one layer all together in some areas of earth. Some even have grass in their mouths, suggesting that their demise came suddenly (in a great flood). No doubt they all lived at the same time.

Another discovery pointing to a sudden and vast flood is the fossil of a whale, 80 feet long, standing vertically on its tail in Lompoc, California, suggesting its being encased in more than 80 feet of mud very suddenly, where it was fossilized. We know that death had to happen quickly, or the whale would have fallen over. It had to be encased in mud or it would have rotted and deteriorated in the atmosphere. It would take a huge flood to move the amount of mud needed to surround a whale.

In another area, 10,000 dinosaurs all died intact. This area also had to be encased totally in mud or their fossils would have dissipated in the elements. One dinosaur found was 70 feet tall and 140 feet long. Again, it would take a lot of mud to encase that one. There exists evidence of 100 to 200 feet of mud in some areas as a result of the great flood. Yes, there was a mighty flood; everything points to it; the Bible is true; you can stake your life on it. God, who is dependable, inspired the Word.

CHAPTER THREE
HEALING MIRACLES

We now think about the reliability of God from a healing standpoint, starting with Miss America 1980. Cheryl Salem was the victim of a terrible accident at age 11. She required over 100 stitches in her face and ended up with one leg much shorter than the other. Becoming a devout Christian at 14, she was in constant prayer for healing.

At age 17 she was told she could never have children because her back and hips were so out of line. Later, however, she was completely and miraculously healed in an evangelistic healing service. Her crippled body was so completely healed that she became Miss America of 1980, competing with all the many other top beauties of America.

Cheryl is now married and ministering full-time with her husband, Harry Salem, and their 3 children. Miracles of healing are the ordinary workings of God. The Lord does all things well. Her gripping story is told in her book, *A Bright Shining Place* or on her cassette tape, *The Music and the Ministry of Cheryl Salem.*

The Bible is a miracle book from a miracle-working God. It is nothing for Him to do the unnatural. He can do so at his choosing. A fitting illustration of this truth involved a Baptist church in South Dakota. It blew up near worship service time, but because of God's providence, 20 or more regulars were each and every one detained from being there, saving their lives. Talk about God's love and His guardian angels!

This miraculous event was on national news, and one of the nation's leading magazines ran a full story on it. The article explained in detail the miracle situation that detained each person. The television show, *That's Incredible,* later published an article on the marvel, a one in a hundred chance for each person of the 20 being prevented from being present at explosion time. But the odds on all being detained at the same time would be 2 thousand to 2 million. Some could say that this phenomenon was only a chance happening, but those involved would never agree. Only one who wished not to be confused by the facts would discredit the validity of the report.

Surely all those involved were right with God for Him to keep His promise of Psalm 91:9-12 "If you make the Most High your dwelling–even the Lord, who is my refuge–then no harm will befall you, no disaster will come near your tent. For he will command his angels concerning you to guard you in all your ways; they will lift you up in their hands, so that you will not strike your foot against a stone." God not only rewarded these faithful ones then, but will reward them even more in heaven.

A Miss Baxter, who was born with a stiff, curled-up body, prayed earnestly that the Lord would heal her. She was a radiant and dedicated Christian in prayer, Bible study, and obedience. One day while alone, she received a revelation from her Lord that on a certain day, at a certain time, she would be healed. When she excitedly tried to tell her mother the good news, her mother smiled, "Yes, I know. God revealed it to me while I was driving on the other side of town." The daughter requested a new dress for the occasion, and her mother bought it. Since Miss Baxter had informed her church of God's promise to her, a goodly number were present at the appointed time.

At the exact time, as promised, a bright, white cloud appeared, but she wasn't healed until the Lord in the cloud touched her. Now perfectly normal, she travels throughout the country giving her testimony in churches. She has even given her testimony on the TBN television network. What God did for Miss Baxter, He can do for you if you love, obey, and follow Him. But He doesn't always choose to heal.

My favorite miracle-healing story is that of Betty Malz. While on a Florida vacation with her family, Betty developed a terrific pain in her side. The doctor diagnosed the problem as her appendix and warned that if it burst, the pain would subside for a short time (which did happen), but she would still have the illness more dangerous than before. But his schedule being full, Betty was not treated by the first physician she visited. Yet the pain persisted and she consulted a second doctor. He disagreed that her problem was her appendix so did not operate. She flew home to Terre Haute, Indiana, where she was again admitted to the hospital. An operation proved the first doctor's diagnosis was correct, but by then peritonitis had developed and her inner organs were disintegrating and filled with gangrene.

Betty was critically ill and in a coma for 44 days, but she could hear and think clearly. Most of her time was spent praying and reflecting on God in her life. Songs rang through her mind, two of which were *The Old Account Was Settled Long Ago* and *I Have Been Born Again*. Though very sick, she was thankfully relieved by the assurance that she had "settled the account" at age 13 and was right with her Lord.

One day during that time, her Uncle Jesse, who was getting off work, had a deep conviction that he visit her immediately in the hospital. He even felt that he shouldn't even go home to shower. Upon his arrival, he learned that Betty needed B negative blood immediately, or she would die. His blood was B negative, so he gave her a direct transfusion, saving her life. God knew Betty's situation, of course, and gave her uncle an emergency revelation. May this true account remind us always to be sensitive and obedient to the unction of the Holy Spirit. A short time after the life-saving transfusion, a man, whom Betty had never cared for, visited her and read to from the Scriptures such as Psalm 107:1, 17-20. Verse 20 says, "He sent forth his word, and healed them; and rescued them from the grave." Betty took these words as God's promise for her healing.

A little later, pneumonia set in to compound the already dire illness. She died for a period of 28 minutes, during which time she had a perfect spiritual body and climbed effortlessly up a long, green, grassy hill, alive with beautiful flowers on the left, which was all very vivid. It was like forever spring. On the right was a wall layered in gem stones, and about the 11th up was topaz, her November birth stone.

She realized a tall, tall angel, dressed in white, was beside her and had always been there since she had received salvation in the Lord at 13 years of age. They communicated by thought transfer, and she was able to understand each of the many languages she heard, which she took in faith for God's healing her.

Betty and the angel came to a beautiful wall with a gate of solid pearl. Melodious music, the like of which she had never heard before, was drifting over the wall, and she joined in the singing.

The angel touched the gate, and it opened. Betty went in and saw the brilliance of the light of God with Jesus on His right. She realized she was in the presence of God Himself. It reminded her of 1 John 3:2: "When he appears, we shall be like him, for we shall see him as he is." Her entire past life passed before her. She was hearing the other end of prayers as they came in and were answered, including her father's beckoning one-word prayer, "Jesus." There's power in that one word, "Jesus." The miraculous love of Jesus!

Retracing her steps, she passed again along the green meadow with flowers now on her right and the wall on her left. She saw the city of Terre Haute, the church steeples, then the hospital, each floor down to the third and in room 336, her body with a sheet over it. Then she was popped back into that body, like an elevator jolts to a stop on the bottom floor.

The heat of the sun shining through the window on the white sheet over her body felt so good. Ivory letters were appearing above her about two inches high. They spelled out John 11:25 as if Jesus said to her, "I am the resurrection and the life. He who believes in me will live, even though he dies."

She threw the sheet off and sat up in bed, scaring the attending nurse. Betty was completely healed and very hungry. She asked for a good meal but was told she couldn't eat because her intestines were disintegrating. Finally, however, the staff relented and agreed she could try a few sips of 7-Up to start with. Soon a nurse showed up with a two pork chops dinner, which Betty devoured with great enjoyment.

Suddenly, a lady came in the room from across the hall, very upset and looking for sympathy from anybody who would give it. She had been given 7-Up for her going-home meal! When the nurses realized the mistake that had been made between the two rooms, they rushed in to pump Betty's stomach, but she refused to let them. She was released in two days. This was all in God's plan to prove that He had healed her completely, even to the point that she has a great love for all people now.

The doctor warned Betty not to have children because her uterus was damaged, and this condition would cause the child to be deformed. Nevertheless, she has a beautiful daughter, normal in every way. Her name is April. Yes, 10 thousand times, the Lord does all things well!

Betty had to die to learn how to live, that is to live the true Christian life of Christ's love. Her miracle has been told via television, and she has a book and a tape titled *My Glimpse of Eternity* that present the details.[6]

Claimed out-of-body experiences, wherein a person's spirit is separated from his or her body, are highly controversial, yet unmistakably clear to the claimant. Many people who have such experiences report being able to think of thousands of things at once in face of great danger, such as heart-stopping conditions where the patient sees doctors and nurses working on one's own body from an overhead position. Other reports claim seeing a light at the end of a tunnel, going to heaven, being in hell, having premonitions of death, and seeing one's life pass before them in a moment.

I had the fast-thinking experience at a very young age, caused by great fear. All I had ever done or thought passed before me in a moment. Now at age 82 and looking back, I believe that it was my spirit, partially apart

---

6. M&M Communications, P.O. Box 564, Crystal Beach, FL 34681

from my body, doing the thinking. Had it been my brain, the chemicals and electrons would have taken time to work it through, for with the brain we think of only one or several things at a time. But my experience was a miracle of body and spirit working together.

The next evidence of out-of-body experiences are the many reports of those in emergency rooms, on operating tables, or in intensive care units when their heart stops and they are out of their body. At first they are up near the ceiling, seeing the doctors and assistants working feverishly to revive them, sometimes even trying to get their attention to tell them they're all right. But the human body in no way can detect the spirit body.

I have talked with several people who have experienced this phenomenon, sometimes called a near-death experience. The massaging or pressing the heart to start it working again is quite common in our time. Some have even told the physicians details of what happened while they were in such a state, happenings they could in no way know otherwise. This is clear evidence that we have a spirit, or are a spirit, and our body is like the clothes we wear or the car we drive. In a sense, our spirit is our inner body. Strange as it may seem, these related facts prove we are both body and spirit and that the spirit continues to live, even when the heart stops. Many people who have had these experiences tell of going through walls or even through people in hallways as a spirit. Admittedly, these are difficult to understand, but the reports are too numerous to be labeled all false. If the heart is not started immediately and the death process lingers, many report going through a dark passage with a brilliant light, pure and white at the tunnel's end, which some have recognized as a person of great and permeating love, even Christ Himself. Some, on the other hand, theorize it to be Satan, disguised as an angel of light, deceiving people's spirit. One's whole life can be flashed before him in a second.

Some see friends and relatives who have died. In one reported case, a man saw his mother, who died at his birth. After being revived, he was shown a picture of his deceased mother, and she looked exactly as he had seen her in the afterlife experience.

Though these sequences are not always in the same order, there are many similarities in the reports. In some cases, people have gone directly to hell, reporting fire, raining firebrands, demons, ridicule, and many more torments. Oftentimes the reported experience was much worse than anything experienced on earth, even to the extent that the affected did not care to discuss it. Their main interest was in getting themselves right with God.

I am well aware that this type of talk is not popular in today's world, but it's very doubtful that all such reports can be wrong. Some claim a heavenly experience so fantastic that they do not desire further life on earth and are very glad to discuss what was revealed to them. Numerous ones remark that the afterlife is much more vivid than life on earth.

Life on earth is only a preparing and proving ground for people whom God can trust in His eternal heaven. Jesus said, "Not everyone who says to me, 'Lord, Lord,' will enter the kingdom of heaven, but only he who does the will of my Father who is in heaven" (Matthew 7:21). God knows that a true born-again person loves Him and will do His will. I believe when we get to heaven, we will not sit idle for the many years (eons) of time in eternity, but will be doing lots of things, maybe jobs or helping angels or even have some God-delegated influence (I have no idea what). But because we truly love God (those who don't will not be there) as His born-again people, we will totally dedicate ourselves to doing His good will.

As a far-out possibility, I suggest–only as an example of some of our heavenly responsibility–that of keeping the planets in order and heaven pure morally. The untrustworthy ones could cause the earth to run into the sun or out into space, or even cause heaven to deteriorate morally. This was the reason Satan was expelled from heaven, as emphatically recorded in Isaiah 14:12-20.

One thing for sure, we must be honest, not injecting our little pet theories of how we'd like heaven to be, but accepting God's way of regulating heaven in His righteous and just manner. We cannot change a thing. He gives us limited insight of our future home in the Bible, especially in Christ's teachings, and now through resuscitation. But we'll never know it all until we get there.

It could be somewhat like my first trip to Alaska. I had read about the state, seen many pictures of it, and even had a great desire to go there, but I really did not know what it was like until I arrived. The thing that was so different about that trip, compared to the heavenly one, was my not having to listen to Satanic theories about it, like those being injected into the afterlife to justify sin and bypass God and His plan. There's one thing for sure, which is that we cannot take our sin with us into heaven. It will not work. The entire universe could be muddled. It's not just a minor mistake; the whole universe is at stake. It's of total importance. God's way is the only way to keep it right. He is the one and only all-knowing, great and awesome God of the universe! One cannot fool God.

Numerous books and articles have been written on the afterlife and out-of-body experiences, which turn many of us off or give us the wrong picture. This is not always intentional. In one person's writings, all of the data used was collected from those who had the experiences up to 50 years before. Thus, mostly the good experiences were remembered, not the bad ones. One author stated there were no negative experiences; then later in his book, he wrote that a woman died, and because of her husband's great love and loneliness for her, he committed suicide to be with her. But he went to an awful place, not at all where she dwelled happily. This was a contradiction in the book. There really is an awful place, and the name of it is hell.

Also there were so many false theories worked into that book that I discarded it, only to regret it later. I now wish I had it in order to expose the fallacy of the theories. Some writers theorize about hallucinations, drugs, hypnotic influences, reincarnation, and other theories to fit their biases, trying to explain away the odd experiences. But we should seek the truth, no matter what.

CHAPTER THREE

The Bible is–by far–the best source of truth. Maurice S. Rawlings, M.D. is a heart specialist who gets his data straight when a patient of his is resuscitated. He hears more hell experiences than heavenly ones. Most of those who have hell experiences either forget or refuse to discuss the next day what they saw.

Dr. Rawlings works with other doctors who use treadmills–with monitors attached–to check a patient's heart under stress. Occasionally a heart stops under pressure, necessitating cardiopulmonary resuscitation (CPR). One such person, a mail carrier, cried when revived, "I was in hell; don't let me die again." His request required the continuous pushing of the rib cage, an action refused by most because of the terrible pain. But for him, it was much better than the hell he was enduring when his heart stopped.

Dr. Rawlings, not a believer at the time, gave the usual comment, "Keep your hell to yourself; I'm trying to save your life." But privately, he knew that he was dead-serious by the horrible grimace on the patient's face. Again his heart stopped, requiring resuscitation, and again he vowed he was in hell.

Then he said, "I can't go back there; what must I do to be saved? Please pray for me." The physician thought to himself, "I'll get him off my back with a make-believe prayer." So he instructed the man to say after him, "I believe Jesus Christ is the Son of God." There was no response, whereupon Dr. Rawlings repeated, "Go ahead and say it." His command was obeyed. The doctor continued, "If I die, keep me out of hell." The man repeated the phrase, then, "If I live, I'm on the hook; I'm yours forever!" Then the man's heart stopped again, but the grimace was gone because he was in heaven. Amazingly, the man lived and is a devoted Christian to this day. The make-believe prayer not only convinced this person; it convinced Dr. Rawlings also.

Later when this person was asked to repeat his experience in going to hell, he either couldn't remember or chose not to talk about it. This is one reason, at least, why most writers on the subject say there is no hell. The witness either dreads to relive the awful remembrance, or–like a woman after childbirth–soon forgets.

Dr. Rawlings, who has authored several books which I highly recommend, now often keeps a tape recorder handy, using it to record a true experience as it happens, or the true story with no mixed-in theories.[7]

It would take an encyclopedia to cover this subject completely. Even knowing all there is to be known concerning the afterlife, however, will not save one from hell or usher one into heaven. Satan knows this better than any of us because he is spirit and can see spirit, but still he is headed for hell. But from all I've heard about heaven from those who have glimpsed the afterlife or have read in the Biblical account about its beauty and glory, heaven is much better than the best of earthly living. Even those who saw life beyond the grave preferred it to remaining longer on earth, yet they bowed to God's will and became more dedicated than ever to His will and in

---

7. *Beyond Death's Door*, first published by Thomas Nelson, Inc., July, 1978. *To Hell And Back*, Thomas Nelson, 1993. Both by Dr. Maurice S. Rawlings, M.D.

His service. I'm told–through hearing and reading from eye witnesses–that heaven's beauty and wonder, plus being with Jesus, is worth a lifetime of suffering the worst possible pain, humiliation, ridicule, and deprivation, should such be demanded.

Earthly life averages 80 years, but heaven is forever. Since the soul is indestructible, it will be in heaven or in hell for all eternity. If in heaven, there will be a glorious existence beyond description. But if in hell, it will be worse than the worst of earth, according to Matthew 13:49-50: "This is how it will be at the end of the age. The angels will come and separate the wicked from the righteous and throw them into the fiery furnace, where there will be weeping and gnashing of teeth."

The "gnashing of teeth" in hell's horror is declared also in Matthew 8:12, 22:13, and 24:51. This indescribable suffering is also attested to by those surviving the experience, if they will even talk about it. There are many more references to hell in the Bible, a subject very important to Jesus during His earthly ministry.

Most, if not all, people who are brought back from trips to hell, immediately get right with God and describe the afterlife as being much more vivid than life on earth. I would never take the chance of ignoring hell and spending eternity there.

CHAPTER FOUR
THEORY VERSUS FACT

Modern beliefs, in relation to ideals, morals, and even physical science, are often theories, at least in part. In some groups such as cults, the beliefs are only notions or wild dreams. It is permissible to dwell on a proven principle, but accepting an unproven theory can be detrimental, even devastating.

I was made acutely aware of this some 15 years ago while polishing my motor home in a California trailer park. A casual friend on crutches stopped by to chat. He made a remark about President Jimmy Carter's giving or turning over the Panama Canal to Panama.

I replied that probably his Christian convictions and principles motivated his doing that. Harvey (fictitious name) blew up, castigating me for even thinking of Christian principles in reference to the president's action. All the while I was aware that everything Harvey was saying was unproven theories. He ended his tirade with, "I am well educated; I have a shed full of books

CHAPTER FOUR

and have read everyone of them." I answered, "Harvey, your trouble is that everything you've said and all those books in your shed are just unproved theories. Am I right?

After a moment, he replied, "I guess you are right."

Then I began relating to him the many parts of the Bible that are proven today. My casual friend admitted I was right, saying that he had never thought of it that way before. He even acknowledged that God did exist and that the Bible is true.

Later as we became good friends, Harvey said he was reading the Bible but preferred worshiping in his own way, not actually accepting Christ in his heart. Even though his visiting nurse took him to revival services in her church, and I talked at length with him, I'm not sure he ever totally committed and surrendered himself to Christ. His reluctance reminded me of taking a shower with a raincoat on or just tolerating God instead of accepting Him, and therefore, not reaping the potential blessings.

I put Harvey on my prayer list. A year later he thanked me. His van caught on fire while he was driving it on the highway, filling the inside with flames, yet he miraculously escaped. In relating the incident to me, he gave God and my prayers credit for his being spared injury. His good fortune was graphically burned into his heart and mind because of a similar happening near the same time in the same area. Two people were burned to death. Harvey definitely felt that God had intervened and saved his life. Despite my having lost track of him, not knowing whether he is alive or dead, I still pray for him daily.

This episode alerted me to the dangers of wrong theories. Harvey had a shed full of them. Scholars, working on their doctorates, are expected to write a thesis, which often turns out to be only an unproven theory. Some of the theories later become proven facts, greatly benefitting mankind. However, one must guard against those theories that are merely pet peeves or are written from a biased and improper motive. Not all literary works are truth.

Also many books propound erroneous theories. An extreme example of this is Adolf Hitler's theory in *Mein Kamp* of a super race (his own Aryan race). This falsehood resulted in the death of millions in the concentration camps and on the battlefields of World War II. May the Holocaust ever remind us to study each ideal thoroughly for its credibility, never accepting and following mere hearsay.

The Bible has been tested and proven from every angle–history, archaeology, fulfilled prophecies, science, and experience. The Bible, down through the ages, has been the anvil that has worn out many hammers. Jesus said, "Heaven and earth will pass away, but my words will never pass away" (Mark 13:31; Luke 21:33). After more than 1,900 years for the New Testament and more than 3,500 years for the Old Testament, the Bible is still with us–and is the best-selling book in the world. About 1970 a psychiatrist wrote in the monthly paper of the

CHAPTER FOUR

Reformed Church, "If everyone went truly by the Bible, we wouldn't need any psychiatrists." The Bible has a solution for solving every personal, moral, and social problem, especially if we use Christ as our role model. The song that says, "More like the Master I would ever be," states it well.

Jesus said, "I tell you the truth, until heaven and earth disappear, not the smallest letter, not the least stroke of the pen, will by any means disappear from the Law until everything is accomplished" (Matthew 5:18). The Bible is a sure answer to our problems and is not outdated as many would have us believe. The new theories often leave us a long way from the right way.

Each psychiatrist and even some psychologists have their own variation of theory of what will work in counseling, teaching, and handling problems of depressed and confused people. Nowadays, books are written expressing a theory which each writer thinks will sell, or espousing his theory of life as he would like it to be.

Schools change theories every few years on discipline, effective teaching, curriculum, and morals in their reading, math, and science books. Many of these theories are exact opposites of one another, so many have to be wrong, or at least, better or worse than others.

Such guesswork resembles the way some car and appliance technicians ply their trade. Instead of locating the problem and solving it, they blindly start attaching parts until they stumble on to one that happens to correct the defect. Often this haphazard procedure is a waste of functional parts when a true diagnosis would have saved much in parts and labor. Sometimes the original parts were faultless, and a correct adjustment of oil would have prevented or corrected the problem and prevented an expensive repair bill. How admirable is the mechanic who has the knowledge and concern to find the problem first, and then correct it.

Similarly, in our society we mishandle our children, young people, and adults instead of molding them by using proven basics. Millions of dollars are spent to correct problems created by bad theories when the teaching of basic principles would have prevented the problem. Our homes, schools, social life, courts of law, and even the government are run on theories, and it's time to return to basics. Let us wake up to the truth that we are dealing with people's lives, not machine parts.

In effect, we are teaching young people through television and pornography to be lawless; then we put them in prison for committing crimes against society. Shame on us! The cost? Twenty-five thousand dollars per prisoner per year for billions of dollars, when simple Bible basics could prevent some of the crime.

Honesty forces us to admit that juvenile delinquency began escalating in the 60s when the Bible, prayer, and the Ten Commandments were forbidden in our schools. It's high time to get back to basics because without them, lives are being wasted, our national debt is soaring (over $5 trillion), and our nation is facing bankruptcy. It will take many generations to pay our nation out of hock.

CHAPTER FOUR

So what is basic? There are basic master gauges in Washington, D.C. of each measurement. Consider the one-inch measurement. The original is really the only perfect inch. Using a replica each time a measurement is made will result in the last measurement showing quite a difference from the original. Going back to the basic standard is the only way the replicas can be trustworthy. However, if everyone tries to make what he thinks (theorizes) an inch to be, or should be, the reproduction would be nowhere near the true inch.

This illustrates what we are doing with our lives today. Let's assume that the true one inch represents the right way of life for society. One idea (theory) of life is lying; another is stealing; another is cheating; another is sex sin; another is drinking; another is adultery; others are dope, graft, folly, and on down the line.

No, society didn't decay all at once, or even in one generation, but through a series of self-pleasing thoughts that seemed harmless at first. But such thinking caused society (spiritually and morally) to drift far away from life's true basics, as does the replica of the basic inch.

Jesus is serious about this principle in Matthew 18:6-7, "But if anyone causes one of these little ones who believe in me to sin, it would be better for him to have a large millstone hung around his neck and to be drowned in the depth of the sea. Woe to the world because of the things that cause people to sin! Such things must come, but woe to the man through whom they come!" This–in effect–is exactly what we are doing by allowing all this damnable teaching to continue in our society. Even Jesus nips sin in the thought stage in Matthew 5:27-28, "You have heard that it was said, 'Do not commit adultery.' But I tell you that anyone who looks at a woman lustfully has already committed adultery with her in his heart." This is a sure way to keep ourselves out of trouble. Remember that an ounce of prevention is better than a pound of cure.

Today's world is filled with greed, hate, and desire for a life of ease and thrills. We are living on borrowed money, creating a national debt which will take many future generations to liquidate. In fact, our present craze for the abundant life is actually borrowing from our great, great grandchildren.

About 1982 one analyst estimated each year's deficit to be equal to the amount that tax evaders cheat the government per year, not counting the amount politicians rake off for graft and payoffs. Making matters even worse, this sad truth exists for most countries of today's world. Our national debt is now over $5 trillion, and consumes most of the collected taxes and the annual interest, yet not enough seem to care about considering the dangerous trend and the consequences.

Mark my word, the day of reckoning is coming with harder times than we've ever imagined. Laugh now, but our present life style will prove to be just another theory that was without validation. Common sense cries out now for basic living. Our current lack of foresight and frugality will put future generations living, possibly, even below the poverty level. We are kings for a limited time. We have unsafe schools for our children to attend now that we have abolished the Ten Commandments, forbidden the Bible's being read, and outlawed prayer in our school system. Humanism has replaced God-ordained morality. This is not only true in what is taught scholastically, but the resultant atmosphere is producing unbelievable criminal behavior. Reports are that some of today's textbooks are too vulgar to read on television, on the radio, or in public.

Why should we be so anti-Bible? Even in Hungary and Russia, which we understand to be mostly atheistic, the Bible is used as literature. It also contains valuable history, good stories (parables), and a proven way of life morally. Humanism that's now being taught in our schools is an unproven theory that is not working, but making vandals out of students. The public schools in America are now waging a battle for the minds of boys and girls through humanism, pursuing a course far removed from the basics of honesty and brotherly love.

Drive-by shootings, raping on school grounds, teen pregnancy, and guns in school have become the order of the day. Our world is full of hate–separating races, families, localities, and many groups of people. The results is bloodshed, riots, rebellion, and terrorism like the Oklahoma City bombing several years ago.

Gone are "the good old days" when most people didn't lock their houses; many didn't even know where their key was. Definitely, we are far away from basics, and as a result, prisons have become an overflowing business, costing billions.

We now boldly live lives of drinking, taking dope, filling the X & R-rated movie houses, watching soap operas, engaging in gambling, enjoying pornography, thinking nothing of promiscuous sex, committing adultery, cheating, and stealing. We do these or watch it on television or the Internet or hear it on the radio. Add to this the reading of pornography as entertainment. We wallow in this immorality and gross sin (at least in thought); then we wonder why crime and vice of every kind rampantly run throughout the land. Immorality has become, more and more, the accepted, normal way of life because of untrue theories, based on selfish desires.

Most of the new theories on social problems are about cure and not prevention, yet we all know that prevention is more valuable than a cure. And lives lost through dope addiction, prison, suicide, and murder are gone forever, never to be brought back or cured.

Today's society forbids our advocating prevention and teaching true basics, despite the rising numbers of young lives being wasted in prison. It's heartrending to witness the apathy of the American public toward our country's moral plunge to judgment. And judgment it is–in this life as well as in the life of eternity. If sin's (unworthy theories) dreadful and final results were apparent to the participant from the beginning of his downward journey (spiritually, morally, and even physically), there would be a lot fewer people gaily and thoughtlessly participating.

The wise practice physical hygiene, cooperate in available immunization, purify water, destroy mosquitoes, and eat nutritious foods to prevent certain illnesses. They dress properly to prevent frostbite, sunburn, or sunstrokes. Moving parts in machinery and appliances are lubricated for a few preventative cents rather than risking hundreds of corrective dollars later on because of neglect. The same truth covers doctor, dentist, and hospital expenses. In these areas, hardly anyone ignores the necessity of maintenance, only to pay the ultimate by not using the ounce of prevention protection.

Yet this is exactly the opposite of what we're doing with our lives socially and morally, especially our young people, often because of parental negligence. We–in reality–teach our youth (and others) vice, wrongdoing, immorality, hate, sex crimes, greed, cheating, drinking and using dope by allowing all this, and more, to be aired on television and to be seen on pornographic movie screens and other mediums as if it all was the right and normal way of life. Instead of teaching, through precept and example, the exemplary life style, parents allow their children to fall into the sinful syndrome of "anything is acceptable if you want it and can get away with it." Contrariwise, basic truths should be taught, and a morally saturated atmosphere of prevention should be constructed over and around these "adults of tomorrow."

But instead, we let our unsupervised young people grow up like wild weeds, condemning them to the courts, jails, and prisons. Sometimes they are unpunished for wrongs committed because of the penal institutions' being already filled to capacity. Loopholes in the laws, or unconcerned and unjustified leniency, also contribute to why punishment is not forthcoming. Then we wonder, "Why? What happened? How did we go wrong?" It is reported that many rapists and sex offenders have their living quarters filled with pornography. The offender is to blame, to be sure, but so is the provider of the obscenity, and so are we citizens of our communities for allowing it.

Remember, Jesus warns that if anyone causes any of "these little ones" (weak ones) to sin, it would be better for him to drown in the sea with a millstone around his neck.

It is mandatory that we get away–right now–from bad theories, which often contradict themselves, and return to solid and true basics, thereby being honest with ourselves and the will of God. It's time to repent and return to Christ and God.

The Israelites would backslide morally every few generations, only to repent and get back on track. Let us have the same enthusiasm for the basics of right as did our Lord and His disciples who walked with Him and saw His mighty works and heard His spellbinding teachings. And what did these disciples do? They only turned the world upside down from glorifying Satan to magnifying the Lord! So can we, but we have to stop moral decline in the thought stage, as Jesus taught. Do not forget that a drunkard started with one first drink, before which he probably fought the drink temptation for a long time before succumbing. Benjamin Franklin once said, "Let no pleasure tempt thee, no profit allure thee, no ambition corrupt thee to do anything which thou knowest to be evil; so shalt thou always live jollily." So let us not slip back and give in to questionable morals by thinking, "I'll buy that. Sounds good to me," or saying the "everybody's doing it" excuse. Remember that "Everybody" will not serve your prison time for you; neither will he go to hell for you. Since you must stand on your own two feet, it's best that you begin to practice right living now. The Lord will help you, if you will let Him.

Due to its continuous, unaltered spread, more needs to be said about the effect an "open-to-all-evil" policy has on our children, tomorrow's adults. We are responsible! We leave the pit uncovered, and when our youth fall into it, their calamity is our fault. Again I say, shame on us. The equivalent is planting seed to grow a garden of men for prison. How, pray tell me, can our young people know what is right when everything around them is wrong! The spiritual and moral environment of our day is like a cancer eating away the very life from our nation. Leading people astray is, in my opinion, one of the worst sins we can commit. Not only does it cause havoc in society, but it puts people on a path leading to hell.

Yet Jesus, in His great love, cares for prisoners, as well as hungry, thirsty strangers. He said, "I was in prison and you came to visit me" (Matthew 25:36). Classifying Himself–in love–with the lowly, He declared, "Whatever you did for one of the least of these brothers of mine, you did it for me" (Matthew 25:40). Verses 41-43 continue, "Then he will say to those on his left 'Depart from me, you who are cursed, into the eternal fire, prepared for the devil and his angels.'" "For I was hungry and you gave me nothing to eat... in prison and you did not look after me." Jesus, in all His great love, puts Himself on the same level as prisoners and the unfortunate.

Jesus had some very strong and definite condemnations for those who do not care for others. It is time to clean up our moral environment that is presently teaching people to be criminals, and in its place, start giving them basic Bible principles of morality by which to live. Believe me, it works.

When a nation's morals are broken down, the nation begins to decline morally and soon falls because she is vulnerable. History verifies that enemy countries often direct their propaganda toward corrupting the morals of a nation to soften it for defeat. Is the same happening in this country, or your country, wherever you may be?

We must get back to basics. There is little time left. Our safety, our society, our nation, and our world are in trouble. We've departed from the firm foundation on which this nation was built, from which we–a growing but struggling nation of only 13 colonies–fought a strong and settled nation (England) for our independence 156 years later and won! We must return to the old ways that we may become strong again.

How scary it is that AIDS is reaching epidemic status, yet mostly through illicit sex, we keep right on spreading it. We have exhausted our great, great grandchildren's energy source and left them an inheritance of a $5 trillion national debt. Chemicals have polluted many of our lakes, given us unsafe drinking water, and produced acid rain. Another great concern is the mothballed Russian nuclear submarines in the North Sea, which could contaminate much of Europe when they deteriorate and the fallout spreads. Dope is available and is used by many young people from the eighth grade up. Gambling has become widespread on all levels.

If we're as wise as I think we are, we will start caring about the sad state of things and begin cleaning up our act before it's too late. We must get back to basics and stop seeking excuses and blaming our problem on our parents and our God. It's our responsibility; it is a commandment from God.

We expect perfection in our appliances, electronic equipment, automobiles, and consumer goods. The space shuttle *Columbia* had to be near perfect or it would not have worked. Shouldn't we expect as much as we relate to others socially and morally? Does it make sense to take death-threat chances with AIDS and other venereal diseases of illicit sex? Do we dare make our children suffer because of adultery and divorce? How insane we are in frying our brains with dope or destroying our reasoning power with alcohol. What a shame and tragedy is our abusing loved ones and committing all the other abusive and dangerous acts of sin and violence.

Theoretically, we do what we want and expect the best from others. An attitude of "I'll do what I want, regardless of the consequences" is just asking for trouble and being tabbed a spoiled brat. If consequences of sin were immediate, we would probably be much more careful about our habits. These are things for which we discipline our children. Perhaps the problem is that we have not matured. There is nothing basic about some of us, but thank God, not everyone is that way.

What is life's true basic standard of rectitude? Where do we start? What are the real truths? What has been proven? Whether we like it or not, we must confess to knowing that every people, tribe, colony, island, or country, no matter how small or how isolated, has a sense of a higher power. It is said that no missionary or explorer has ever found any tribe or group of people who didn't have some kind of god to worship and look to for help. This report is not popular with those who attempt to ignore any thought of God, passing it by, or explaining it away, like an obstinate child.

Many people make their own gods out of gold, brass, ivory, stone, or wood, but using plain common sense, we know these are not any kind of gods at all. They cannot see, hear, or respond. They are lifeless. But worshiping inanimate objects is nothing new. We are as guilty when we make material things the god that we, in actuality, worship.

Just about everybody prays to God in a near-death experience, like in a foxhole during war. Most everyone has a sense of afterlife, heaven, hell, spirits, both godly and Satanic. Evil spirits have been thought to dwell in old, abandoned houses, which we refer to as "haunted houses." We, as Christians, have the power to remove them in the name of Jesus.

CHAPTER FOUR

We've thought about gods, but now let us concentrate on the true and living God of the whole world. What is He like? He is awesome beyond imagination–a super power, a great creator, an all-knowing One, able to be everywhere all at one time (omnipresent), loving, perfectly just and true beyond description. He created the entire universe, millions of light years in diameter, and in comparison, we are as electrons in size, compared to God and His universe. There are millions of electrons in an inch. Jesus said in Matthew 10:30 that even the very hairs of our heads are numbered by God. I believe if the Bible were written today, it would say the molecules of our body are numbered because God knows every atom, molecule, and electron by name.

We people are so tiny in comparison to God and His universe, which He created. Still some of us ignore Him, blaspheme Him, try to boss Him, worship and obey Satan, saying God doesn't exist and all in the universe just happened to evolve. Nonsense! We cower to a man one inch taller than we are, yet in effect we shake our fist in the face of God, who is greater than His whole universe. How stupid can we get! I want to be on God's side, no matter what! His Word, the Bible, is the only true answer to the solution for a way of life. And it's not theory but proven fact (for those who have their eyes open).

The holy Bible is inspired by God and has been tested and proved in every possible way for 3,500 years. God has revealed Himself as our awesome God, telling us what His will is for our lives in a true and basic way that works–if you use it. His Word only cleanses and blesses when it is applied to the heart and life. Even a lot of us Christians have body odor because we do not use God's cleansing power.

It is alarmingly true that church after church is quitting God and joining Satan and the world. Oh, they are still sitting on the corner of Main Street and there's lots going on, but it is not of God. Unknowingly, they have turned the church and themselves over to Satan. They are a social society rather than a house of prayer, fasting, and worship. Some have stopped really teaching the Bible; others are teaching the Bible's very opposite. They leave the supreme One out, yet they call themselves His church. They are wolves in sheep's clothing and should be (and will be) shunned by the true, born-again child of God. Those of God-given discernment can quickly detect the false places of so-called worship. Let us not despair, but remember that each of us is individually responsible and has to answer for himself. Jesus said, "Not everyone who says to me, 'Lord, Lord,' will enter the kingdom of heaven, but only he who does the will of my Father who is in heaven" (Matthew 7:21).

Let's be totally honest with God and ourselves, not letting our selfish wants persuade us. What did Jesus teach us by example? On the night of His betrayal (by Judas) and His arrest, He prayed, "My Father, if it is possible, may this cup be taken from me, yet not as I will, but as you will" (Matthew 26:39).

The genuine Christian will always pray the unselfish prayer of what is best for others, his nation, and the world, and for God's will to be done in us and "on earth as it is in heaven" (Matthew 6:10). And we do this out of deep and grateful love for Him.

Let us not forget that life on earth is a testing ground for people, especially Christian people in every part of our lives. Persecution is to be expected, and it will surely come to the dyed-in-the-wool, dedicated one who determines to follow God through His Word and the Spirit. Yet it is through suffering for righteousness sake that we grow; therefore, we accept it as an opportunity and obligation. The fact is that we even glory in it, as did the beaten apostles (Acts 5:41).

The football player gets knocked down in practice, but it prepares him for the upcoming game before a stadium full of people. The harder the coach drives the team member, the better player he becomes. Only by hard preparation through practice is the athlete able to last through the contest, contributing to the team's success. No matter how much we suffer, or in what way, it will never equal the suffering of Jesus during his crucifixion.

Jesus didn't have to come to earth; He could have remained in heaven, which was thousands of times better than anything on earth, but His great love for us drove Him to earth so we could escape hell. Have you thought about this? God cannot allow anyone into heaven who He cannot trust. Remember, it was for this very reason that Satan was expelled from heaven. God couldn't trust him, and neither can you. God knows that the born-again child of God loves Him and will gladly do His will in heaven as he does it on earth. Nevertheless, our sin debt still had to be paid. Prisoners of the state pay in years of separation from society, but Jesus suffered agonizing pain, humiliation, and ridicule and labored to pay the penalty that we should have paid. He died the cruel death of the cross, an invention of the Romans that is only exceeded by hell in its victims' suffering.

Christ's death not only paid the penalty for our sins, but gave His own a reason for loving Him and doing His will. In that act of love, Jesus was fulfilling 1,400-year-old prophecies proving his deity as the promised Messiah (Son of God). Honesty demands that we admit we will never suffer like Christ did during His crucifixion on the cross unless we go to hell. Its suffering would be worse.

But Christ died that heaven would be our home, not hell, and He did it all in love, as taught in John 3:16: "For God so loved the world that he gave his one and only Son, that whoever believes in him shall not perish, but have eternal life." What a tragedy it would be if all the suffering and dying Jesus did for you should prove to have been for naught because of your rejection of Him. Accept Him *now* as your own personal Lord and Savior. You'll be glad you did.

Before Jesus came to earth, the world wondered what He would be like. They asked, "What can we expect from God's Messiah, Son of God, Savior, Lord? Will He be for the rich, or the super strong, or will He be smart? What about the poorest of the poor? Jesus answered those questions, according to God's purpose in sending Him, by being born in a stable and cradled in a feed trough (manger) for animals. Since God is sovereign, the birth of Jesus could have been any way God desired. God chose an humble birth and a sacrificial life for His Son so He could relate to all human beings. God's Son would be no respecter of persons, as Peter explained in Acts 10:34-36: "God does not show favoritism but accepts men from every nation who fear him and do what is right. You know the message God sent the people of Israel, tell the good news of peace through Jesus Christ, who is Lord of all."

So salvation is free to everyone who accepts Jesus as Lord and Savior. It is not something bought because that could cause many of the very poor to lose out. And that would not do because Jesus loves us all.

As the One of lowly birth grew into boyhood, He did manual labor as a carpenter until He was 30. He had no wealth, as He said in Matthew 8:20, "The foxes have holes and birds of the air have nests, but the Son of Man has no place to lay his head." He was crucified for a crime He didn't commit. He was ridiculed and spit on, and buried in a borrowed tomb. He endured all this, proving His ability to understand our problems.

I am reminded of the man who tried to get a bird to come in out of the bitter cold. He thought, "If I could only become a bird, then I could persuade the bird to cooperate." Suddenly it dawned on him that Jesus, in principle, did just that. He became one of us in order to relate and explain the great truths of earth and heaven. Then when dying for us on the cross, He even prayed for those torturing and killing Him by saying, "Father, forgive them, for they do not know what they are doing" (Luke 23:34). Jesus is our Savior because He is the only one who ever qualified for the assignment. Not only did He pay our penalty for sin, but He fulfilled every prophecy concerning the coming of the Messiah. Also He who was without sin, went to the cross as a lamb to the slaughter, yet without bitterness or unforgiveness toward those who took His life. His dying between two thieves and in the stead of Barabbas, the criminal, adds to the evidence for His qualification to understand and save mankind. But perhaps the biggest reason He qualified to understand our problem and produce the remedy for our sin was due to His being God and the creator of all things, thereby licensing Him to make the rules of salvation. His humbling of Himself and becoming obedient unto death, even the death of the cross, in no way diminished the reality of His awesome deity, glory, power, and love as the triune God of the universe.

One of the greatest things Jesus ever did in His earthly ministry, in my opinion, was His washing His disciples' feet at the Last Supper. His act was not like ours on Maundy Thursday (the Thursday of Holy Week, commemorating Jesus' Last Supper) because we wash clean feet, feet cleaned in bathing for the special service anticipated. Instead, Jesus washed feet that had walked dusty roads, even where horse droppings had been left, and they were dirty and smelly. In this act, Jesus was doing the work of a slave and identifying Himself as one. But His loving act taught His followers, who would carry the torch after His death, and showed us what we should do and the attitude we should have toward one another and the poor. Christ did not only tell them; He actually did it. This self-denying act is recorded in John 13:1-9: "It was just before the Passover Feast Jesus knew that the time had come for him to leave this world and go to the Father. Having loved his own who were in the world, he now showed them the full extent of his love. The evening meal was being served and the devil had already prompted Judas Iscariot, son of Simon, to betray Jesus. Jesus knew that the Father had put all things under his power, and that he had come from God and was returning to God; so he got up from the meal, took off his outer clothing and wrapped a towel around his waist. After that, he poured water into a basin and began to wash his disciples' feet, drying them with the towel that was wrapped around him. He came to Simon Peter, who said to him, 'Lord, are you going to wash my feet?' Jesus replied, 'You do not realize now what I am doing, but later you will understand.' 'No,' said Peter, 'you shall never wash my feet.' Jesus answered. 'Unless I wash you, you have no part with me.' 'Then Lord,' Simon Peter replied, 'not just my feet, but my hands and my head as well.'"

When Peter realized the lesson Jesus was teaching, he wanted all that his Master had to offer. He was not interested in being lukewarm; he wanted to be hot (all-out) for Jesus in true love, as we all should be. This love should bubble over into helping the poor, homeless, orphans, sick, handicapped, and prisoners. There never was a prisoner whom Jesus didn't love. He was crucified between two of them.

Let us never forget that a trickle of departure from God's ways can turn into a torrent of sin that will put us too, in prison, in want, and in ruin. All of us make mistakes and need forgiveness. Jesus said, "Whatever you did for one of the least of these brothers of mine, you did it for me" (Matthew 25:40).In His great love, Jesus classes Himself with prisoners. That's how humble the Savior of the world is.

Like an earthly father, God–through Jesus Christ–had a logical family plan for salvation and eternity. Christ, as head of the family, loved us so much that He left perfect heaven, suffered the ultimate, and died on the cross to pay the penalty for our sins. That is somewhat like a father paying his son's fine, or taking the blame for a crime his son committed–even to the point of serving that son's prison sentence.

If the son appreciates it, loves his father for such an unselfish act, and rewards his father by mending his ways in total love, he will still be a part of the family, probably much closer than before. In like manner, if we appreciate and love Christ for suffering on the cross in our place and invite Him into our heart and life, God (seeing our sincerity) will know that He can trust us in His heaven and will enter our lives for now and ever more. Then we too will have a home for all eternity in heaven with the family of God.

Remember, earthly life is less than a second of time in comparison to eternity (the hereafter), which is forever and forever–and that's a long, long time. Christ, because of His love and grace, is like that father who would suffer in the place of his son. Jesus said, "Watch out that you are not deceived. For many will come in my name, claiming, 'I am he,' and 'The time is near.' Do not follow them" (Luke 21:8) At least 60 have come claiming to be the promised Messiah, and there are some 2,000 cults in the world, besides idol worshipers and the like. Christ is saying here that many will claim to have the way of salvation and the ticket to heaven. And the religious situation of today confirms the truth of His foreknowledge of our day. This is only one of His many prophecies of future events. The Bible contains many more.

Of Christ's predictions, a favorite of mine is Matthew 24: 24: "For false Christs, and false prophets will appear and perform great signs and miracles to deceive even the elect." Is this happening today? Yes. Many humanistic and Satanic churches are trying to displace Christ. God grant that we all will choose to be one of the elect.

On another occasion, our Lord said, "Love the Lord your God with all your heart and with all your soul and all your mind. This is the first and greater commandment. And the second is like it: 'Love your neighbor as yourself.' All the Law and the Prophets hang on these two commandments" (Matthew 22:37-40).

God knows if we truly love and trust Him all the way, and if He can trust us to be in heaven with Him. It makes sense that God cannot have people in heaven He cannot trust, running the risk of their fowling up heaven like they have His world. And what a mess mankind has made of His world! The verses above are a basic rule by which to live, not just a theory. Just think what the saying of Jesus really means. Why, our entire court system, if it were honest and true, could operate on these two laws.

We now look at other proofs of Christ's identity as the promised Messiah:

1. People who lived with Jesus Christ saw His miracles, heard His teachings, and witnessed His resurrection. They were so sure of His Messiahship that nothing, including persecution and death, could stop them from proclaiming Him as the world's Savior. Chased hither and thither, they still proclaimed the Christ out of undying love, and His gospel was spread like wildfire. They knew what they had received, believed, and preached was basic fact, not just unproved theory.

2. The four gospels of Matthew, Mark, Luke, and John, which record the life of Christ on earth, are surprisingly alike in detail. This indicates the truth of the gospel story. Written by four different people with four separate views of Christ's life, they are more accurate than the report would be from four people, standing side by side, reporting an automobile accident. Theory? I think not. John said, as he concluded his gospel, "Jesus did many other things as well. If every one of them were written down, I suppose that even the whole world would not have room for the books that would be written" (John 21:25). Don't explain The story away. It is true basics.

3. Another concrete proof of Christ's validity is the complete about-face of Saul of Tarsus, later to become Paul the apostle. Zealously serving the devil in an effort to wipe out Christianity, Saul was struck by the brilliant light of Christ Jesus, talked with Jesus personally, was endowed with the Holy Spirit, and became so fervent for Christ that he stopped at nothing in proclaiming Jesus Christ as Savior and Lord. More than once Paul was beaten and left for dead, only to come up preaching the very doctrine he had once sought to destroy. He even performed miracles in Christ's name, after his conversion. He spent a lot of time in Roman prisons, but utilized the time in writing five of his circa 14 letters to the saints. Those letters–so richly inspired by God–became books of the New Testament, enabling Paul to greatly extend his faithful and fantastic ministry. His prison epistles are believed to be Ephesians, Philippians, Colossians, Philemon (*The Student Bible, NIV,* Yancey/Stafford, Zondervan Publishing House, `86, `92, `96). It is also evident that 2 Timothy was penned from his final incarceration in Rome, where he was beheaded for being a Christian.

It's amazing what Jesus can do in changing the human heart! This transformation is happening daily in prisoners' hearts as they rise from complete madness to trusted citizens. Prisons all over the U.S. and in many other countries of the world are open to the gospel because it works. It is basic fact, not theory. True satisfaction in life is forgetting oneself to consider others in giving, in sharing, witnessing, helping, caring, feeding, ministering, comforting, and doing for others in compassionate love. What motivates this type of life? The unselfish love of Christ while He sojourned on earth among humankind, not telling but showing them (and us) how to live the worthwhile life. Jesus taught us to live for others, expecting nothing from them in return, but assuring us that such a life would be richly rewarded in heaven. Unselfishly helping others helps us forget our own stress, and that's basic therapy that works.

Dr. Albert Schweitzer, M.D., was probably among that distinguished group of happy and fulfilled persons who dedicated (and dedicate) themselves to the work of God. Schweitzer was a missionary doctor to Lambarene, Africa, where he remained until his death at 90. He was gifted, educated far above the average, and could have become financially rich in America. Yet he chose to spend his life–from 38 to 90–working for next to nothing in Africa and even building the Schweitzer Hospital on the Ogooue River, where thousands of Africans received treatment. He, along with Mother Teresa, will have many treasures in heaven.

Paul advised Titus, to remind the people [at Crete] to be subject to rulers and authorities, to be obedient, be ready to do whatever is good, to slander no one, to be peaceable, considerate, and to show true humility toward all people. The Cretan Christians were to remember that they too were once foolish, disobedient, deceived and enslaved by all kinds of passions and pleasures. They–along with all humans–had lived in malice and envy, were hated and hated others (Titus 3:1-3). No one is perfect, except Jesus, but that is no excuse for our not following Paul's admonition just given. We must be forgiving toward all if we want to enjoy our forgiveness.

Let's be sensible. We wouldn't jump off the Empire State Building just because someone said, "Everybody is doing it," would we? If we did, we'd surely suffer the consequences because each of us must answer for himself. Like it or not, every step we take we obey God's gravitational laws by stepping to keep our balance and not fall to the ground. Neither should we defy God's laws for living and His will for us. Such defiance leads to corruption and trouble in our lives and in our nation. Where do we stand in our country? Does the shoe fit? Are we following good basics, or are we on a theory tangent?

We expect and have perfect television, and automobiles and airplanes for–most of the time–perfect, pleasurable service. Yet our morals are anything but good, and through TV programs, X-and R-rated movies, pornography, and vile music lyrics, our children are exposed to that which will cause them great trouble. Shouldn't we strive for perfection in our moral lives also? We are leading our children and weaker ones astray. I have a friend who says, "Of all the privileges afforded me, the opportunity to be a good person is my top priority."

A mother deer will fight off a dangerous predator to protect her fawn, putting her own life on the line for her offspring, but today mothers and fathers alike put their own lusts and pleasure first, before their children. This selfishness often leads to divorce. The children, who should come first, because they are their parents' own flesh and blood and of God, are not given justly deserved consideration. Remember also that they did not ask to be born; we brought them into the world, and they are our responsibility. They also are the future generation of this world. What can we expect if we neglect to give them right principles–or any at all–by which to live?

The question is asked in Proverbs 31:10 "A wife of noble character, who can find? She is worth far more than rubies." Today's sex-filled advertisements, talk shows, movies, soap operas, pornography, legitimized abortion (which astounds the mind and conscience), and the excessive emphasis on birth control methods have altered many if not most of our women's minds to the point of aspiring to be sex symbols rather than worthy mothers. Women–because of their foundational position in life as well as their strong influence in the molding of their children's lives–should aim toward being mother symbols, not sex symbols.

Although men are not excused in this matter of family morality, women as mothers are generally much closer to our children. If the mother is virtually basic and godly, the children have a much better chance of growing up well-established citizens. Let us not forget that the hand that rocks the cradle rules the world.

Mothers, you have a very important responsibility pertaining to the kind of adults your children will become. But the rest of us must also accept our responsibility in this matter of developing moral integrity in the lives of succeeding generations. An immoral poison surrounds society and challenges us all to steer clear, maintaining clean minds and setting the right example for our young people (the adults of tomorrow) to follow. Society's moral decline of today can justly be placed on all of us because truly, children are everyone's problem and responsibility.

A virtuous woman is a greater jewel than ever in this immoral environment. Some psychologists and other teachers theorize that the present decadent spiritual and moral conditions make no difference in human behavior, but that is a lie of the devil. Ted Bundy, the rapist and serial killer, blamed pornography totally for the path he traveled. Had it not been available, the probability is strong that he would not have chosen a life of crime and sin. Our hearts break over those who elect to destroy innocent victims, denying them their God-given privilege of living and developing. Even though the Bundys pay for their crimes, I cannot help but wonder how the pornography providers will feel when they answer for themselves in their time of judgment.

Deuteronomy 13:4 says, "It is the Lord your God you must follow, and him you must serve. Keep his command and obey him; serve him and hold fast to him." This Scripture admonishes us to shun listlessness and apathy while being on fire for God, walking after the true Lord. Jesus said, "Can a blind man lead a blind man? Will they not both fall into a pit? . . . Why do you look at the speck of sawdust in your brother's eye and pay no attention to the plank in your own eye? You hypocrite, first take the plank out of your eye, and then you will see clearly to remove the speck from your brother's eye" (Luke 6:39, 41, 42).

These words of Jesus move us to purify our own lives so that we may qualify to help others walk the straight and narrow path, to the glory of God. Christ commanded, "Be perfect, therefore, as your heavenly Father is perfect" (Matthew 5:48). A true, Christ-like principle to live by is: God's perfect will first; then man's will, machined to precision by the Word of God.

In Matthew 5:21-22 Jesus speaks of the judgment day, "You have heard that it was said to the people long ago, 'Do not murder, and anyone who murders will be subject to judgment. But I tell you that anyone who is angry with his brother will be subject to judgment." This, again, is basic prevention in strong language. This truth says to stop crime in the thought stage before someone is hurt This is a rule of Jesus, and His rules are not to be taken lightly.

Most modern entertainment puts sinful, violent thoughts into our minds. 1 John 3:15 says, "Anyone who hates his brother is a murderer and you know that no murderer has eternal life in him." So it is mandatory that we clean up our entertainment and thought life, not diluting or explaining away the commands of our Lord. Following Him even in this regard brings peace of mind, satisfaction, happiness, and health to the participant. The saddest thing about hate is what it does to the hater. It is well known that hate produces stress, which doctors confirm can even cause cancer.

CHAPTER FOUR

Some of our contemporary preachers say that they cannot preach the true gospel (in certain instances), or just lightly gloss it over. Such omission is a terrible mistake. As previously mentioned, to cause "one of these little ones" to sin (err) is worse than having a millstone hung around one's neck and being cast into the sea, or it would have been better not to have been born.

This type of talk only emphasizes the impossibility of dodging the results of sin. Again, our Lord's words were sure and stern. We must never, in any way, be the cause of His chosen ones going astray. Let us get away from "off the cuff" sermons and preach the straight Word of God, thereby keeping our lives in line with His will. Let's get down to basics.

Jesus spent much of His time warning scribes, Pharisees, priests, and other religious leaders of their sins and short comings. And He warned the people of the religious leaders in saying, "Be careful . . . . Be on your guard against the yeast of the Pharisees and Sadducees" (Matthew 16:6)–who were false prophets–and their non basic behavior.

In Matthew 7:15-17, 19-21 Jesus warned, "Watch out for false prophets. They come to you in sheep's clothing, but inwardly they are ferocious wolves. By their fruits . . . you will recognize them. Likewise every good tree bears good fruit, but a bad tree bears bad fruit . . . Every tree that does not bear good fruit is cut down and thrown into the fire [eternal hell]. Thus by their fruit you will recognize them. Not everyone who says to me, 'Lord, Lord,' will enter the kingdom of heaven, but only he that does the will of my Father who is in heaven." Check it out, read it all for yourself. It is from our Lord Himself.

And here is more! Do not tolerate sin. Our Lord will be the true judge. Read the Bible. Be informed. Know the truth. Don't wait for eternity to discover what truth is. Five seconds after you die, you will know the truth for sure, but then it will be too late. The devil already knows, and because of the truth he cannot escape, he trembles.

Pray every day for a great awakening in our nation and world. Get back to the Lord. Get back to basics. Let this revival begin with you and me. Our Lord will help us to Him if we will only earnestly ask in believing faith. Never underestimate the power of prayer. Now is a good time for a 24-hour prayer and fasting vigil. It's high time for some basic action.

Let's not do something for which we will be sorry. Even in Sweden, as in most nations, where illicit sex has been grossly oversold, the very ones who first advocated sexual irresponsibility are, I am told, now very sorry and want to turn back to purity of sex and marriage. Loose sex now poses even a graver danger because of the rise and spread of AIDS. Promiscuous sex now could definitely be one's death sentence.

There's a familiar saying that one rotten apple will spoil the whole bushel. This leads us to shun bad company, keeping our bushels (lives) free of rotten apples, lest the whole (of life) go down the drain. A good, but dangerous application of this thought is all churches uniting under one head–and being led astray. Another application is giving money to churches that support hate groups. We should never get into something we can't get out of, such as gangs, the Mafia, or even despotic government. Once in, as with quicksand, there's no way out, but in a casket. The dogma of these groups is theory, not basic truth.

Jesus said, "Everyone who does evil hates the light, and will not come into the light for fear that his deeds will be exposed. But whoever lives by the truth comes into the light, so that it may be seen plainly that what he has done has been done through God" (John 3:20-21). This certainly makes sense to me.

1 John 4:20 says, "If anyone says, 'I love God,' yet hates his brother, he is a liar. For anyone who does not love his brother, whom he has seen, cannot love God, whom he has not seen." Never hate anyone because each person is God's creation, and a beneficiary of Christ's death on the cross, as were we, but to be one's Savior, Christ must be accepted into one's heart out of love for Him..

We should never try to get revenge on someone since it accomplishes nothing but the committing of two wrongs–the one on us, and the other by us. But the main reason for not getting back at someone is that it is forbidden by God. "Do not take revenge, my friends, but leave room for God's wrath, for it is written, 'It is mine to avenge; I will repay,' says the Lord" (Romans 12:19). And He does. Our Lord has done it for me more than once. This is truth that has worked from the beginning of time, admitted by anyone who has looked at the subject honestly.

My mother often said, "Two wrongs don't make one right." Taking her advice, let us not get caught up in the "I don't get mad; I get even" syndrome. This attitude is a lie of the devil. I've heard this expression used many times–sometimes even in a proud, self-righteous manner–by Christians who often did not realize the seriousness of what they were saying. Others made the "I get even" remark just to be funny. However, a Christian or a clergyman should never use this phrase or run down another Christian behind his back just to hurt him. The same holds true for denouncing a denomination because of one person or church within it. Such does not show Christ-like love for Christian brothers or the Lord's church. This type of slander hurts both the church body and God's kingdom. It stirs a hate attitude amidst the entire congregation.

Don't get even; forgive. That's the right thing to do. Forgiveness has many times more power than getting even. After forgiving the adversary, pray for him.

Let us pray, earnestly and unceasingly, that people all over the world, and especially in the United States, will turn from hate, greed, and sins of all kinds–starting a great and new awakening, a worldwide revival, the likes of which have never happened before. This can surely happen if we will humble ourselves, forgiving and repenting, as stated in 2 Chronicles 7:14. If every world citizen were a born-again child of God, there would be no need for prisons, courts, lawyers, police, armies, and war equipment. Taxes would drop over 50 percent. The cost of one prisoner is $25,000 per year and there are millions of the incarcerated, so the cost of government would plunge.

This desire sounds impossible, but it is merely the Great Commission of Christ's last command to His disciples: "Therefore, go [because all power is given to me in heaven and in earth], and make disciples of all nations, baptizing them in the name of the Father and of the Son and of the Holy Spirit, and teaching them to obey everything I have commanded you. And surely I am with you always, to the very end of the age" (Matthew 28:19-20).

God desires us to have a great compassion for souls, a love so great that we do not want even our worst enemy to go to hell. Many worst enemies have become best friends by accepting Christ as Lord and Savior, which (if the conversion is real) completely changes the heart and makes a new person out of the former one. This has been proven often and is very basic, not just theory.

Regarding forgiveness versus revenge, Romans 12:9-21 reads, "Let love be sincere. Hate what is evil; cling to what is good. Be devoted to one another with brotherly love. Honor one another above yourselves. Never be lacking in zeal, but keep your spiritual fervor, serving the Lord. Be joyful in hope, patient in affliction, faithful in prayer. Share with God's people who are in need. Practice hospitality. Bless those who persecute you; bless and do not curse. Rejoice with those who rejoice; mourn with those who mourn. Live in harmony with one another. Do not be proud, but be willing to associate with people of low position. Do not be conceited. Do not repay anyone evil for evil. Be careful to do what is right in the eyes of everybody. If it is possible, as far as it depends on you, live at peace with everyone. Do not take revenge, my friends, but leave room for God's wrath, for it is written: 'It is mine to avenge; I will repay,' says the Lord. On the contrary: If your enemy is hungry, feed him; if he is thirsty, give him something to drink. In doing this, you will heap burning coals on his head.' Do not be overcome by evil, but overcome evil with good." Proverbs 25:22 adds, "You will heap burning coals on his head, and the Lord will reward you."

Herein are some of the Bible's best verses on forgiveness. They are also informative about getting along with people, especially Christian brothers. Furthermore, the teaching of these verses are proven basics; they are not unproven theory.

Considering all the evidence of God's sureness, His Word, the Bible, soul, spirit, heaven and hell, I am overwhelmed with, "Wow! What an awesome, mighty, powerful, loving, passionate God we serve." Then turn to His great creation, just from the beauty aspect. View the pheasant, cardinal, and wood duck. In flowers we thrill at the rose, carnation, tulip, and others all around us. Then there's the sunfish and all the many other beautiful species of fish. In fact, there are so many great beauties of our world and universe that it would take a whole book, all by itself, to cover them. I could never, never believe that all these wonders in beauty and detail just evolved from absolutely nothing.

The theory of evolution is just that–a theory. It isn't basic, and it isn't truth. To contend that every molecule, atom, electron, proton, element, light ray, and much more evolved is to say that they had to evolve before life could have evolved. How long would it take for the first electron to evolve? A million years? Since electrons do not reproduce themselves, it would take another million years to develop the second, which wouldn't work exactly like the first. There are millions of electrons, I'm told, in one inch. The universe is full of them and they all must work together, precisely alike, or we would not have electricity and all the other things in which they are active. So who but God could set up nature in the first place!

And heaven? I am compelled to believe from all the evidence that heaven is many times more beautiful than the best earth has to offer. Another poignant point is that we are here on earth only some 80 years, on the average, but God's children will be in heaven for billions of years, yes forever and forever.

So in our Christian love, we should have a deep passion for souls, eager to tell everyone about our Jesus and His saving love. We should cringe at the thought of even one soul perishing in the fire of hell. The Great Commission, if obeyed, is a basic plan that works in this realm.

But are we like the lad who said, "I want to do it myself," disregarding God's basic plan and laws for every learning experience and process? The little boy represents those of us who want to disregard God's plan and rules, doing it our way. But that only proves disastrous, as taught in Proverbs 14:12: "There is a way that seems right to a man, but in the end it leads to death." Why do people refuse to accept Christ and salvation? Is it because they do not want to go by God's rules, but prefer to make their own?

THEORY VERSUS FACT PAGE 95

Why do we try to salve our conscience by attempting to explain God and His kingdom away? Whether or not we have agreed to it, we go by God's law of gravity every step we take, or we fall flat on our face and suffer the consequences. But fellow pilgrim, wake up! All of God's spiritual laws are equally important. Obey them and live. Ignore them and die (spiritually). Such reasoning is not theory, but absolute, sure, and basic truth.

CHAPTER FIVE
WORKING TRUTH

It is universally known that an automobile requires oil. If the oil's warning light on the vehicle's dashboard activates, the motor must be shut off immediately or there's great trouble ahead. Without oil, it takes only five seconds to five minutes–at the most in today's close-tolerance engines–to burn out every bearing in the motor. Yet an oil check at the last service station stop could have prevented the inevitable breakdown. Likewise, proper moral training can prevent the deadly effects of rape, murder, robbery, dope overdose, and their kin.

Automobile owners also know that failure to grease the steering, suspension joints, and wheel bearings causes them to wear out before their intended time, resulting in a costly repair bill, or even worse, a bad accident. Improper lubrication invites a drag link to come off or the loss of a front wheel while, on the other hand, if properly greased, their faithful performance can be counted on for possibly more than 200,000 miles.

CHAPTER FIVE

In the same way gradual, unsuspecting flirtation with moral impurity can lead to moral failure. Unchecked pornography leads to rape, child abuse, sodomy, adultery, and other sex crimes and X-and R-rated movies lead to robbery, murder, bombings, dope addiction, and drunkenness. Remember the alcoholic did not suddenly become a drunkard; his problem began back with his first drink. And such travesties scream to the world for the moral oil of prevention.

A frog dropped into hot water will quickly jump out to safety, but if put in cold water that is slowly heated to a boil, the frog will not notice the change in temperature and will boil to death. This is how subtly pornographic movies, and even suggestive advertisements work on us—bit by bit—to drop untold trouble in our laps.

Consider television, for instance. We accept obscenity, essentially, when we first begin watching off-color TV programs. At first, their filth is like dew and mist, but they gradually affect our thinking and spirituality like gentle rain that later turns into a torrent. We, without realizing it, drift little by little in thought and behavior until, alas, some of us even wind up in prison because of our lack of moral and lawful restraint. If the consequence of these gradual sins were more obvious, there would be fewer victims. In effect, we are teaching our youth to commit immoral acts; then we put them in prison for it.

Today's society, as a whole, is becoming more morally and spiritually bankrupt with each passing day, as our newspapers and other news media testify and confirm.

The trend began in the early 60s when prayer, the Bible, and the Ten Commandments were removed from our public schools. I have a preacher friend who has been a pastor and Christian minister for 52 years. He can recite from memory all the books of the Bible in one breath and quote several of the Psalms word for word in their full length. In what church did he learn that? He didn't. He was guided in it in the weekly devotional period of his seventh grade class in public school in Texas in about 1940.

I declare that the change toward secularism is not working, or is working backwards. How sad it is that our schools of 1999 are not safe for our children. How can we expect them to know what is right when everything around them is so wrong.

We've been thinking on what doesn't work; now we turn our attention to what does. Jack Murphy (Murf the Surf), Harold Thompson, and Don Holt once topped the list of undesirables in the United States. Jack, a world champion surfer at one time, stole some of the world's largest jewels out of a museum in New York, for which he was given two life sentences, plus 20 years, never to be returned to society. Harold Thompson robbed 11 banks, was sentenced to 105 years, and sent to Alcatraz in San Francisco Bay. Don Holt, from Oklahoma and a hardened criminal, was sentenced to 500 years of prison life.

But all three convicts accepted Jesus Christ as Lord and Savior while behind bars, and He turned their lives around. Through the miracle of conversion, the never-to-be-free-again threesome were returned to society and have been out of prison 10 years, 24 years, and 17 years, respectively. All three have gone from being the most distrusted to being completely trustworthy. In fact, if I had to send all my money in cash to one of my children and there was no other way to achieve that but through one of these three men, I would not hesitate in giving any one of the three the assignment. Christ in one's heart produces the miracle of transformation. Such can be compared with a ruined motor, run without oil, being suddenly made new again by a power beyond human explanation.

The Sandi Fatow story is another example of God's changing power in a person's life. She was a moll of the underworld and a heavy user of drugs, had her Zodiac sign tattooed on her body, but had never known a minister of the gospel, and knew nothing about our Lord Jesus Christ.

Sandi, under the influence of drugs and on a mission for a friend, went to a Christian rehabilitation center but was admitted herself as patient. After 18 hours of such exposure, Sandi decided those around her were a bunch of stupid squares, but something else was happening. The effect of the narcotics she had taken began wearing off, giving her a painful withdrawal reaction.

In order to get the drugs she craved, she had to go by way of the center's assembly area to get outside the building. She had to pass through a prayer meeting. What she saw in that earnest group impressed her as being something different and perhaps worth her investigation and consideration–upon her return. However, her plans to leave were interrupted when the group surrounded her, laid hands on her, and prayed for her. Amazingly, Sandi was instantly and miraculously healed of her withdrawal reaction and addiction, and in addition to that, she gave her heart to Christ, becoming a born-again child of God and follower of Him.

She was 23 years of age then; she is 51 now and has been clean ever since. She is happily married to a minister, who pastors a church in Knoxville, Tennessee, and for the past several years Sandi has gone with us on prison ministry weekends, giving her testimony to the prisoners.

Never underestimate the power of prayer to Almighty God. Miracles are simply the everyday, ordinary workings of God, who can and does do them at His will. His miraculous power has worked for literally millions of cases that seemed impossible to change. Preventing is better than curing, which is much better than waiting until lives are ruined or lost. In either case, Jesus is the answer. Does this make sense to you?

If sin's results were immediate, none would get caught up in the sin that slowly causes these catastrophes. True, a sin doesn't seem so bad at first, but step by step it traps one, like the frog floundering in slowly heated water.

Christ stops sin in the thought stage with a warning. For example, hear Him say in Matthew 5:27-29, "You have heard that it was said, 'Do not commit adultery.' But I tell you that anyone who looks at a woman lustfully has already committed adultery with her in his heart. If your right eye causes you to sin, gouge it out and throw it away. It is better for you to lose one part of your body than for your whole body to go into hell."

A recent news report told of a man in prison for child molestation. Having served his time, he was about to be released, but he begged, "Don't let me out because I know I will do it again; I cannot help myself." Then he requested castration to remove his lustful desire so he would not hurt another child. Such a person knows the results of sin, probably caused by pornography. The real cure for such behavior is a change of heart in Christ.

Jesus explained the real oil of prevention that works. If we accept Christ and ask Him to help us, and really mean it, He will come to our rescue. He instructed His disciples: "Watch and pray so that you will not fall into temptation. The spirit is willing, but the body is weak" (Matthew 26:41).

Sandi Fatow says, "When I was born, I didn't say, 'Mama, take me down to the dope house; I want to get some drugs,'" or Jack Murphy did not request when he was born, "Mama, take me down to the jailhouse; I want to serve a little time in prison." It all came about gradually, little by little.

So we need Jesus and His teaching as the oil of prevention. But Jesus is not only to be thought of as a preventative, but the One who can supernaturally bring a person out of the pits of peril as He did Sandi and Jack.

What happened? They accepted Christ as their Lord and Savior, and He changed their hearts. He will do the same for you too. What an awesome, loving, powerful Lord and God we serve! People need the Lord.

We are now privileged to witness the changing power of Christ under the most unusual and dire circumstances. This true story took place in Colombia, South America.

Medellin, Colombia, is considered the most violent city in the world. Bella Vista Prison in Medellin was the most dangerous prison in Latin America, but now God's power is transforming prisoners' lives and bringing hope to the whole nation.

Jeannine Brabon, a missionary and teacher at a Colombian seminary, tells the story.

Medellin is a city where death culture reigns. Sometimes the death toll hits 100 per day. Death is a business, and young lads begin at age 12 earning money by killing people.

Oscar was a young man of 28, who had lived his entire life in poverty. At 12, he took to the streets and soon became a thief just to have something to eat. Being on the streets led to drugs. He was in and out of prison for the next 16 years. He came out of prison and was met by a colleague. Oscar looked at him and said, "You are fat!" meaning he had received enough to eat; he wasn't wasted by drugs.

Oscar said, "What's happened to you? You look different." The man replied, "Jesus has changed my life.

I have come to know Him and, Oscar, He can change your life too." The friend invited Oscar to a small church. Later Oscar said, "The Holy Spirit drew me like a magnet. I found myself at the front of the little chapel, weeping my heart out, and asking God to forgive my sins and come into my life. When I stood up, I was a new man, the 16-year drug habit broken."

Instead of buying drugs, Oscar used the money in his pocket to buy his first Bible. He couldn't read, but he took it home to his mother and she read it to him. This is what the Lord spoke to Oscar on his first day as a Christian. "The Spirit of the Sovereign Lord is on me, because the Lord has anointed me to preach the good news to the poor. He has sent me to bind up the broken hearted, to proclaim freedom for the captives and release from darkness for the prisoners" (Isaiah 61:1). This passage went right through him; he couldn't get away from it.

And so he went back to Bella Vista Prison, from where he had just come, and asked the governor if he could have a pass to go into the prison. The governor said, "No one wants to go into this prison. Don't you know what the situation is?"

Oscar knew. There were between 30 and 60 men murdered there every month. The administration was ready to send in the army; they didn't know what to do. Yet Oscar, one small man, in obedience to God, stood before the governor and said, "God changed me, and He can change any one of these men." The governor's heart was touched. He gave him a pass and Oscar began to go into the prison. He said, "I was a criminal, but I had never seen what I saw there. I had to step over decapitated men. I saw wounds of 200-300 knife stabbings; the situation was absolutely infernal." He had to take a clean shirt [each time he visited the prison] because the prisoners would throw things at him and yell obscenities.

But I prayed God would give me some of the hardened ones, the 'top dogs,' said Oscar, and one by one, men began to come to Christ. One of these, Orlando, had experienced a similar life to that of Oscar. At 12 he became involved in crime and eventually reached the Mafia. He had become a professional killer, termed a *sicario*. He had his own offices in several major cities in Colombia with men working under him, and he could earn $15,000 from one assignment.

He landed in prison and thought, "I am going to commit suicide. I'd rather take my own life than to have someone else do it."

But another prisoner said to him, "That isn't the answer; Jesus is."

Orlando said, "How can I know more?

The man replied, "This little man who comes in here, he will tell you."

So the next day, when Oscar made his entrance, Orlando found him. He said, "I've had everything money can buy, but I've never had happiness." That day

CHAPTER FIVE

Orlando found not a religion but a person, the Lord Jesus Christ. With a small group of these men, Oscar desired to preach in the wings and got permission to hold a campaign.

The day before it started, 13 men were wounded and 3 were murdered, but that didn't deter Oscar. He went in the next day and began to share that Jesus was the answer to the conflict that raged within, the answer to the death toll.

The day he began to preach in the prison, the killings stopped. The press waited outside for the death toll, but there was none that day, or the next. The headline–one year later–in the secular press was: "One Year No Homicides in Bella Vista," and then a full-page report of what God was doing inside the most dangerous prison in Latin America.

It was at this time that I [Jeannine Brabon] was crying out to the Lord, "What can I do?" Oscar had never had any schooling, but his wife had and was studying in our seminary at Medellin. It was through her that I met Oscar, who invited me to the prison. My first day there, Oscar asked me to preach, and I said, "Oscar, who is my audience?," and he answered, "Mostly *sicarios* (hired killers), and not Christians."

About 30 or 40 men came in. Orlando was there––I recognized his face from his testimony in the paper and I just couldn't believe that this was that tremendous killer. I took a passage about King David wanting to show God's steadfast love to someone of the house of the enemy [2 Samuel 9:1-13, which describes David wanting to show godly kindness to a relative of his enemy, the late King Saul], and as I began to share, I sensed the lord's presence there in a very real way.

When Oscar gave an invitation at the end of the message, 23 men stood to their feet with tears streaming down their faces, asking Jesus to come into their lives.

Oscar said to me, "Jeannine, would you help us train leaders?" This man was pastoring more than 300 men behind bars, and from the questions he was asking, I knew he need to be trained. So in February of 1992 the Bella Vista Bible Institute began with 25 men.

Since then, we have baptized close to 300 men. For the men to be baptized, they really have to walk their experience in the wing. It is very hard because they are ridiculed.

They are respected by the guards because everyone knows the peace of the prison is due to the believers, and the other prisoners have been warned, "You don't touch them." In fact, when there is a delicate time, the leaders in the wings come to our men and say, "Get your men together and pray so there won't be violence."

God is using what is happening in the prisons to reach into homes. We have a live radio programme [*sic*] inside the prison, put on by the inmates. They sing, one preaches, they give their testimonies, and I speak, and it is one of the most listened-to programmes. At the close prisoners give greetings to their families, so the families all tune in, and you can see the guards up on the wall listening too. Prisoners' entire families are coming to Christ and the impact on society has been tremendous.

The director of public prosecutions asked to see me, and for an hour I shared with him. Tears streamed down his face and he said, "This gives me hope for the country." And so God is reaching from the lowest in society to the very highest.

It's not easy—Colombia is in a life-and-death struggle and it's spiritual warfare. We live with death threats. We have six missionaries kidnaped by the guerillas. Oscar's brother was tortured and murdered and, when that happens, it's a direct threat. But God is building His church. He is working at a time when the violence has opened people's hearts, and the prison has become the pulpit for the rest of Colombia.

Jeannine Brabon is a member of OMS International, an American missionary organization. Pray for her, Oscar, and the others involved in the work at the Colombia prison. (Her reproduced report is used by her permission).

Let us take a further look at proof that God's plan truly works. First are the miracles performed in and upon lives that were brought from the guttermost to the uppermost through Christ's saving power.

Second is Oscar's being saved unto life eternal, into a meaningful life. He was instantly healed of drug addiction, with no withdrawal pains. Then he felt the calling to preach, was anointed by the Holy Spirit, even though he was limited in education and was not even able to read. But his great love and passion for souls offset that and he had a most effective Holy Spirit-filled witness, despite being derided and having objects thrown at him. Oscar's finding Christ as Lord and Savior of his life reversed the curse that Satan had planted on him.

Oscar was a doer of the word, and not a hearer only. He, like Dwight Lyman Moody (1837-1899), made up for his lack of education with the holy anointing placed upon him by God. Moody, it is said, murdered the English language, but his great love for Christ and lost souls has accorded him a place in history as one of the greats of evangelism. What would he have been if he had been able to use radio and television! My evaluation of this former Chicago shoe salesman, though I never heard any of his sermons, is that he really was a great vessel, fit for the Master's use.

Billy Graham–in one school of his education–attended Florida Bible Institute in Tampa, Florida. While a student there, he felt God's call to be a preacher and said, "Yes" to his Lord. Having a great yearning to preach but no invitations to do so, he began, anyway, for his first sermon. He perfected four 20-minute sermons, practicing from a stump out in the woods. Soon he was given his first preaching opportunity, which excited him to such a degree that he preached all four of them in 8 minutes. But he didn't quit and has gone on to become possibly the greatest evangelist who ever lived. Billy's success in his worldwide ministry has been his dependence on the Holy Spirit and his prayer life, which is the evidence of what really works. May his example be a lesson to our younger preachers and pastors.

I thought at one time in my life that I would be a preacher, so I took public speaking in high school. But finally I decided that I was a total failure as a speaker, so I gave it up. I certainly was not like Billy Graham in perseverance, but now one-on-one prison counseling really works for me.

Remember that Oscar's friend witnessed to him, then took him to his church, where Oscar was saved and healed of drug withdrawal pains.

I feel compelled to ask you a question: Is the church you are attending a true one in every respect? Does it exempt you from feeling unsaved? Is it one that will lead a friend you have invited to church to the Lord? Is it one you can recommend to a new convert for Christian growth? If you honestly have to answer no to these three questions, then that church is not preaching the whole gospel. You not only need to make a change, but there is an urgent need of prayer for that church and pastor.

Oscar's friend was also healed from drug addiction when he accepted Christ. In essence, Oscar's friend was an Andrew. John 1:41-42 tells us about Andrew: The first thing Andrew did [after he followed Jesus] was to find his brother Simon [Peter], and tell him, 'We have found the Messiah,' (that is, the Christ). And he brought him to Jesus. Jesus looked at him and said, 'You are

Simon son of John. You will be called Cephas,' which, when translated, is Peter [stone]. To learn what Jesus meant by "stone," turn to Matthew 16:18: "And I tell you that you are Peter, and on this rock I will build my church, and the gates of Hades will not overcome it"

Peter played a key role in starting Christ's church, which has remained strong down through the ages. We read Acts 2:40-41 from the Living Bible: "Then Peter preached a long sermon, telling about Jesus and strongly urging all his listeners to save themselves from the evils of their nation. And those who believed Peter were baptized–about 3,000 in all!"

Naming Peter *Cephas* (stone) was a prophecy by Jesus about Peter that was fulfilled in a mighty way soon after Jesus had ascended back to heaven.

As Peter was brought to Jesus by Andrew, so was Oscar brought to Christ by his friend, who had found Jesus the Christ. Through that one act, much was done in turning many away from drugs and killings in Colombia, with a rehabilitation program that really works.

What made the drastic change and difference was the prisoners' receiving Jesus Christ as Savior and Lord. It is interesting to note that statistics reveal that 90 percent of the prisoners who genuinely accept Christ into their hearts never return to prison once they are released.

Through the spiritual tidal wave that hit Bella Vista Prison, the killings there sank to zero from 30 to 60 a month. And just think, it was all started by a man who couldn't read. It had to be totally the work of the Holy Spirit dwelling within that person. Praise the Lord; He indeed is awesome.

Before leaving the subject of Medellin, Colombia, let's view a bit more of the life of Orlando. Like Oscar, he was in the drug scene and on the streets by the time he was 12, but he had graduated (or degenerated) to killing for hire as a member of the Mafia. But he realized his sinfulness and was contemplating suicide when a friend said, "Don't kill yourself; there is an answer in Jesus, and Oscar will help you." Orlando lost no time in finding Oscar, who led him to Christ. Again God's plan worked; he was not only saved but healed from drugs with no withdrawal pains. He ceased murdering because he had been eternally redeemed and made new.

Notice what the conversions of Oscar and Orlando accomplished in their place of ministry at Bella Vista Prison in Medellin, Colombia:

1. 23 (mostly *sicarios*) were converted to Christ in one meeting.

2. Killings dropped from about 550 a year to 0.

3. 300 were saved in Oscar's congregation.

4. The stabbings and cuttings were curtailed.

5. Bella Vista Bible Institute was founded within the prison with an initial group of 25, which at the last report was continuing to grow.

6. An effective radio ministry was begun, which changed the moral atmosphere of the city and that part of Colombia for the better.

7. An impact was even made on the director of public prosecutions.

8. The prison governor and guards heard the gospel and were impressed.

God, through His Spirit, accomplished all this through a man who couldn't even read. What miracles! What power! What a working! What a loving God!

Surely Oscar, like all of us, has a very special place in heaven, which Jesus has prepared for him (John 14:2). Jesus said, "I tell you the truth, anyone who will not receive the kingdom of God like a little child will never enter it" (Mark 10:15). A state-wide prison warden in Connecticut announced at one of our prison ministry meetings that he had been a warden in two other states and had seen every kind of rehabilitation program for prisoners–religious and otherwise–but said that nothing works except the prisoners' accepting Jesus Christ as their Savior. Then 90 percent do not return. About 70 percent of the prisoners rehabilitated any other way return to prison in about two years, a fact borne out by the Institution for Prison Ministry at the Billy Graham Center at Wheaton College. So receiving Christ is good insurance for getting out and staying out of prison. Again, it's the only thing that really works. But what about the monetary savings in this type of approach? A study made in the Bill Glass Prison Ministry for six years, at a cost of $23,500 per prisoner per year, estimated savings to the taxpayer was some $3.2 billion. Divided by a U.S. population of approximately 250 million people, it amounts to a savings of about $13.20 per man, woman, and child in the whole country. Now we see where God's plan really works in our pocketbooks.

In 1996 there were 32,000 decision for Christ through the Bill Glass Ministries. Using a round figure, let us assume that each one converted to Christianity will spend one year less behind bars at an average annual cost of $25,000. This would equal a taxpayer savings of $800 million, or more than $3 per man, woman, and child. This is a savings paying big dividends in a program that gets the job done.

Jack Murphy, Harold Thompson, and Don Holt are now out of prison and are completely trustworthy because of Christ's dwelling within them. All three are an important part of the Bill Glass Prison Ministry. Their going straight represents a savings to the taxpayer of more than a million dollars. And this savings represents only three prisoners who were rehabilitated into respectable citizens.

It is credible to calculate that all three of these men could live another 20 years each, for a total of 60 years, at a savings of $25,000. The reason? Because three inmates let Jesus come into their lives to change their hearts.

Remember that this equation pertains to only three transformed prisoners, but in 1997 alone, there were more than 33,000 prisoners led to the Lord (our best year thus far). Realizing it is God who gives the increase, we give Him all the credit.

The Bill Glass Prison Ministry has worked with prisoners for 25 years. Add to this effort that of former associates now working on their own and those led to Christ now leading people to the Lord themselves. This ministry succeeded exceedingly in an Oklahoma prison in 1986. A couple of the converted prisoners gave their all in a burning compassion for souls as they worked with us. When we returned in 1992, we found to our delight that almost all the inmates had been led to the Lord. One inmate said to me, "I arrived here only yesterday, and already two of the prisoners have visited me in reference to receiving Christ.

Totalling the results of these ministries, there is no telling how many have found the lord as Savior through the Bill Glass Prison Ministry. And don't forget the money saved for the state, nation and taxpayers. Yes, this soul-winning ministry has an economic value, it's true, but the most important result is souls saved for all eternity, prisoners rehabilitated, peace of mind, respectable lives, freedom from addiction and vices, and safety for society in the reduction of lives lost through murder.

We must ever remember that Jesus loved the prisoner and identified Himself as one of them when He said, "I was in prison and you came to visit me" (Matthew 25:36), and when pressed for an explanation of these words, He answered, "Whatever you did for one of the least of these brothers of mine, you did it for me" (Matthew 25:40). Come what may, we should all be bubbling over with enthusiasm in telling everyone about our Jesus and being a witness for Him in thought, word, and deed. It is an activity that pays great dividends, changes attitudes, saves souls, and *really* achieves what it seeks. Let's be sensible.

Bill Glass also has a youth ministry and an evangelistic ministry of citywide crusades, both of which are efforts of prevention ministries. Only God knows how many precious lives are spared prison sentences by these soul-saving, life-redirecting endeavors.

How do we evaluate people? Our answer should be that they are souls who need a ticket to heaven. Their souls are without color, handicap, or nationality. With our new body, we will all look the same in heaven.

Today a good percentage of the world champion athletes are born-again Christians: Paul Wren and Anthony Clark, former and present world's strongest men; Bill Chaffin, the basketball star who is in the *Guinness Book of World Records* for spinning 18 basketballs at the same time; plus many others in football, basketball, and baseball. Yes, these world champions are all born-again Christians, despite today's society with its drugs, liquor, sex, crimes, porno, and sins of all kinds.

Many of the would-be top world record sports figures get trapped in vices that rob them of their chance of ever becoming the world champion there were bodily and mentally capable of being. Many even get caught in lawlessness and sent to prison. So generally, born-again Christians are the ones who make it to the top in athletic competition.

Bill Glass was an All American tight end for the Baylor University football team in Waco, Texas, then played 12 years of professional football with the Detroit Lions and the Cleveland Browns. His superb athletic ability put him in the Football Hall of Fame in Ohio. Bill also has a very effective citywide crusade program in which he serves as an evangelist.

An additional ministry is his youth program, Champions For Today. This effort is led by Mike McCoy, an All American Notre Dame footballer who went on to play with the Green Bay Packers, Oakland Raiders, and New York Giants, achieving All Pro NFL player status.

Rescuing youth is the number one need in America today. Violence and immorality run rampant in our society, leaving behind a devastated generation without hope, many even going to prison. But coming to know Christ as personal Savior nips violence and immorality in the bud, that is, in the thought stage.

McCoy, with years of experience in reaching teenagers, has been influential in changing thousands of young lives. Each Champion For Today (CFT) worker is a former NFL player who is specifically trained to address life's issues. Champions For Today pros have spoken all across America in schools to thousands of our students needing to hear the truth of prevention. The main target of the youth program is the public schools.

CHAPTER FIVE

America's young people desperately need to be taught Christian faith and behavior before it's too late. Statistics tell us that 85 percent of those who accept Christ do so before age 18. This oil of prevention is also the best way to prevent our youth from ever serving time in our prison system. We must stop sin's stranglehold on our youth in the thought stage. Christ is the answer. Positives seldom happen by chance.[8]

The efficient Bill Glass Prison Ministry runs on a minimum of resources, something I believe that keeps it in line spiritually, yet it is one of the largest prison ministries of its type in our country. There are eight follow-up sessions for each new believer (with Campus Crusade for Christ guidance) to help him/her grow spiritually after each prison weekend.

More than 90 percent of those never return to prison, and some even get out early, if a change of heart is truly evident. The ministry could enter many more prisons if additional finances and counselors were available. The open doors of invitations are in hand, and it is sad when we are forced to say no. People, especially prisoners, need the Lord.

A missionary in Africa saw everyone in his village accept Christ, resulting in no one being in jail or prison. Think of it! No prison or jail budget. What a cash savings. Truly Christ is the great preventative. In Cook County Jail in Chicago 46 percent accepted Christ in the Bill Glass Weekend of Champions of 1997 with a

---

8. Champions For Today pros will come to your community to give hurting youth the chance they need. Call (770) 963-5097 (phone/fax) or contact Mike McCoy national director, 551 Exam Court, Lawrenceville, Georgia 30244.

crime rate decrease of between 10 and 20 percent for the county. Most impressive! The jail has given the ministry a standing invitation for the second weekend in each September every year, which began in 1998.

Looking at soul-saving from the dollar efficiency view, I believe the Bill Glass Prison Ministry is one of the most efficient missions on earth. Prison is the place where the residents are most hungry for the gospel. When one wishes to pick peaches, he goes to a peach tree, not a pine tree. In like manner, prisoners know that they are at the bottom of life, and that the only way out is up, and Christ is the right way up.

Another significant monetary savings is that for the addict who becomes a child of God. His habit of drugs can run as high as $1,000 per day. Addiction to alcohol costs a minimum of $20 a week, or this can represent a week of one's monthly paycheck, causing the victim to lose his home, health, family, and job. A complete acceptance of Jesus into the heart by those hooked on these expensive habits eliminates the problem by destroying the craving, and even the withdrawal pains. Again, what a financial savings, but the greater recovery is for the life that is saved for the present life as well as the eternal one in heaven.

CHAPTER SIX
NEW LIFE TOOLS

God's people are commanded to tithe (Leviticus 27:30), but many believers refuse to do so. "A tithe of everything from the land, whether grain from the soil or fruit from the trees, belongs to the Lord: it is holy to the Lord." We are to give because we love our Lord, not from an ulterior motive. Our giving should be done cheerfully. Remember you can't take it with you.

Some preach that you will get more back than you give, thus teaching the "give to get" motive. Not so! We are to give in love, not expecting to be repaid monetarily by the Lord. However, it is no secret among His people that God–in many cases–does bless us far above what we give.

We can and should pray for our needs, and God does promise–through His providence and love–their being supplied. This is especially true if those needs are born from an insatiable desire to further His kingdom and help people experience the new birth.

CHAPTER SIX

Some current preachers are preaching that God wants a Christian to be rich, but God knows that some people cannot manage riches. The "health and wealth" theology, claiming that God will make all of His "true" disciples healthy and wealthy, crowds out Christ and salvation. Christ, the God-man on earth, and the Scriptures, God's gracious gift to mankind, were not given to enrich us materially, but spiritually. Earthly riches can be enjoyed in a temporary life on earth, but an investment in the spiritual and moral will be enjoyed in heaven forever and, as an extra bonus, that life will be lived on golden streets.

Jesus said, "Do not store up for yourselves treasures on earth, where moth and rust destroy, and where thieves break in and steal. But store up for yourselves treasures in heaven, where moth and rust do not destroy, and where thieves do not break in and steal" (Matthew 6:19-20). This directive, true and noble as it is, teaches still another great truth: there will be no thieves in heaven. Does not this apply to church members who rob God of His tithes and offerings (Malachi 3:8)? God's true children obey Him.

Give to evangelistic-type missions so everyone can hear about the saving power of Jesus. The last command Christ gave, before ascending back to heaven (from where He came), was the Great Commission, which tells us to share God's good news across the globe.

See how God cares! Even though He cannot allow into heaven people He cannot trust, still He does not want anyone to go to hell (2 Peter 3:9). What an awesome, caring, loving God we have! We've talked about the money saved through those who have accepted Christ as Savior and thereby have become Christians. However, the real significance is: This amount is what sin and Satan have cost us. In trying to rehabilitate the addicted through prison and removing them from society for our safety, our cost is $25,000 per year per prisoner.

This means we are trying to cure a problem after it has occurred by a method that is not working. Convicts return to prison repeatedly, becoming more hardened each time. Actually, what happens in prison is similar to public school offering a course on evil conduct. There is only one answer to our world's crime problem, and that is letting Christ into one's heart. The results will be that 90 percent will not return to crime, some of which will possibly be released early. It's about the only way out.

Early basic Christian training in life, plus a restriction on obscene movies and foul-tongued literature, can prevent this great loss of life and all the wasted years.

Statistics prove that only the Christian type of rehabilitation programs work successfully. In the others, 90 percent do return, with 75 percent going back to prison within three years. The Christ way works both in prevention and in cure–if it is used.

An engrossing account of this very principle is recorded in Matthew 9:20-22: "Just then a woman who had been subject to bleeding for twelve years came up behind him and touched the edge of his cloak. She said to herself, 'If I only touch his cloak, I will be healed.' Jesus turned and saw her. 'Take heart, daughter,' he said, 'your faith has healed you.' And the woman was healed from that moment." God heals us spiritually as dramatically and completely as He healed this woman.

A superlative way that God's plan of salvation works is through forgiveness. First, we must forgive our fellow-man in order to receive God's forgiveness for ourselves. This principle is taught in Matthew 6:15 and was also a part of the model prayer our Lord gave us in Matthew 6:12. Forgiveness is vitally important to Jesus–He said to forgive 77 times [according to the NIV, but the KJV, The Living Bible translation and The Amplified Bible translation understand it to be 490 times, i.e., seven times seventy]. So forgiveness should be important to us, His children. Hate is the usual bedfellow of unforgiveness. The sad thing about unforgiveness is what it does to the hater (the one who will not forgive). Unforgiven hate can cause sickness. Many misunderstand forgiveness. They feel to forgive condones the hurtful or harmful act that was done. It does not. It acknowledges the wrong, but releases the results of that act to God.

One of Satan's favorite sayings (traps) is, "I don't get mad; I get even." But the Bible admonishes that it is the Lord's prerogative to repay a wrong, not ours. We're also advised to forgive and help those who have wronged us. Getting even is forgiving your assailant wholeheartedly, for such a strange reaction will literally blow his mind!

The classic example of forgiveness was related at an early morning prayer meeting that I attended. Our pastor arrived late and explained that he didn't get to bed the preceding night until 1:30 a.m. A jeweler hired an ex-con just out of prison, who had begun stealing at age five. He had been hired by this jeweler to be rehabilitated. Early into the ex-con's employment, the jeweler discovered that a $10,000 diamond was missing. Upon questioning his employee, admission of guilt was confessed and the gem stone returned. The thief thought no doubt, "My boss will notify my parole officer, who will put me right back in prison without even a court hearing." But after a little time and thought the jeweler said, "I'm going to give you another chance." This blew the ex-con's mind.

It was all the forgiven man thought about the rest of the week. Given extra time to think on Saturday, his day off, about what had happened, he finally could handle it no longer, so Sunday evening he went to the jeweler's house to pour out his guilt, shame, and remorse. The jeweler tried to console him but in vain, so the pastor was called about 11:00 p.m. The two talked to this humiliated man for some two hours and led him to the Lord. Feeling his forgiveness with peace in his heart, the employee's problem was settled.

Forgiveness in this instance paid off beyond imagination, for if the store's owner had called the parole officer, as was expected, the man would have been back in prison immediately. And from that time on, he would be in and out of confinement, each time for a more serious crime. The final story of his life could have been a life sentence or even execution. But now he will never, under any circumstances, take even the tiniest thing that doesn't belong to him. And beyond that, he is saved for eternity because God's way of forgiveness works.

Jesus taught us not to look back on what people have done to us. He said, "No one who puts his hand to the plow and looks back is fit for service in the kingdom of God" (Luke 9:62). While you are looking back at what you have done and what others have done to you, you get off the course in front of you, and wind up ploughing a crooked furrow. It's the same in life. When we are looking back at our hurts and hates, we are not doing all we should do in our lives before us, and the distraction affects our witness.

When we stand alone before God in the judgment, we can't excuse our looking back in unforgiveness by claiming we were abused; we must answer for ourselves. We must stand on our own two feet, with Jesus, before God.

Jesus is our friend who will go with us all the way, even to the judgment before God Himself. Have an "I'm not discouraged; I'm heaven bound" attitude. Isn't that what 1 Peter 1:8 teaches? Listen: "Though you have not seen him, you love him; and even though you do not see him now, you believe in him and are filled with an inexpressible and glorious joy." It is a joy from peace of mind because we forgave all and we are forgiven our sins and are heaven bound. It works.

Not only does forgiving shame our enemy; it gives us a calming peace of mind. It replaces hate with love and gives the forgiver a new friend. And we all need every friend we can possibly win to ourselves, but when we forgive as Jesus commanded, He becomes our true friend and He is the greatest of all.

I heard of one person who hated his dad so much, because of child abuse when he was young, that in his mind he dug him up from the grave every morning and beat him up again. This man was still letting his dad ruin his life in abuse even after he was dead. He and all of us should forgive our abusers–whoever they might be–getting them off our backs and getting on with our lives.

Others and Satan can only abuse us mentally if and when we permit them to do so. Through Jesus, we have power over Satan and his demons. So we have to rise above it all, even in this life. Remember, today is the first day of the rest of our lives here on earth.

Another imperative of new life tools is God's Word, the Bible. The best way for people to know about stewardship (tithes and offerings), forgiveness, and all the other great attributes of God's kingdom is having a Bible in their own language.

Wycliffe Bible Translators (WBT) is perhaps the most dedicated and effective organization whose workers translate the Bible into the language of particular communities.

This organization is more interested in the "what" than the "who." It cares not who does the work and gets the credit but is concerned only that every tribe and people

CHAPTER SIX

in the entire world have the Bible in their own language. Wycliffe readily helps other organizations who diligently strive toward making the Bible understandable to all mankind. They put God's work ahead of personal glory and credit.

My prayer is that Bible translation continues to be WBT's chief aim until the job is completed. Wycliffe Bible Translators was founded by Cameron Townsend after he realized that the Bibles he was selling to people were not in the customers' language. It was impossible for them to read what they were buying, so Townsend translated the entire New Testament into the language of the people among whom he had been working. Others dedicated to the lord began helping any way they could–one by one–and the movement became Wycliffe Bible Translators, with a current membership of nearly 6,000 workers spread around the world.

Christian disciples of many other countries and other missions have now started their own Bible translating organizations. Presently more than 450 new Bible translations have been completed by Wycliffe as the organization continues to work relentlessly. Yet the sad truth is that some 3,000 communities of people still do not have the Bible in their own heart language. Many of these are anxiously awaiting the day they will be able to read God's Word.

A classic example of this work's splendor is embodied in Marianna Slocum and Florence Gerdel's going into Chiapas, Mexico, to translate the Bible for the Tzeltal Indians. The full story is told in the book, *The Good*

Seed.[9] The Tzeltal Indians were a crude people indulging in drunkenness and plagued with superstition, sin, cruelty, and a destructive tribal culture. Living in rustic shacks, they were drunk from Friday night to Sunday night of every week in the year. The witch doctor's stipulated pay from the sick was in liquor, and if it was not supplied, he would place a curse on the delinquent family. Schools, clinics, and churches were all but nonexistent. Music was seldom heard, and there was no joy or laughter.

When the two women began their work in Chiapas, the witch doctors and their followers taunted and threatened them. A new church was burned to the ground, and one of the first believers was murdered. However, Florence, an excellent nurse, worked unselfishly to minister to the diseased and injured. Her soothing and healing ministry did wonders in establishing good relations with the Indians and causing them to be receptive to God's work among them. While Florence's ministry blessed the people physically, Marianna was joyously translating the Bible into the people's native tongue.

Soon a portion of the Biblical translation was finished and recorded on a phonograph record. Then the record was played from house to house by new believers, and word of what was happening spread like blazing fire. Hebrews 4:12 explains why: "For the word of God is living, and active. Sharper than any double-edged sword, it penetrates even to dividing soul and spirit, joints and marrow; it judges the thoughts and attitudes of the heart."

9. *The Good Seed*, by Marianna Slocum, Promise Publishing Co., 1988

CHAPTER SIX

The work in Chiapas grew slowly, but it did grow–person by person, family by family, bit by bit. Even a church was organized through Christ's saving power. The two missionaries ignored difficulties and earnestly did their work, finishing the Tzeltal translation of the entire New Testament in about 15 years. Six years later, a translation was completed in the Bachajon dialect, and by that time some 70 churches had been established. Then the two translators moved to Colombia, South America, and spent 20 years translating the Scriptures into the vernacular of the Paez Indians.

On a return trip to their Tzeltal friends, the two ladies rejoiced in finding 322 thriving churches and 50,000 believers, as of May 1985. All of this happened because two of God's servants made His Word comprehensible to a people who knew Him not.

People coming to Christ through the Word have transformed the community. Roads have been built, homes are respectable, schools–with volleyball courts–operate efficiently, and a great sense of community pride exists. And to think, it all came about through the Word of God that was made intelligible to a people for whom Christ died on Calvary.

Yes, the people, armed with God's Word and the Holy Spirit's guidance and power, brought about this great increase in their quality of life. Let us never minimize the power of God the Holy Spirit, the holy Word, and the efficacy of prayer. This is what accomplishes great spiritual and moral victories, and it is the answer to all the world's problems.

Another evidence of Bible translation merit comes from the Ifugao area of the Philippines, where Len Newell completed a translation of the Word into the local lingo. His gift changed for good the entire area, founding some 100 churches with 2,000 believers, but Len did not rest on his laurels. He and his wife moved on to another area with a different language, where they are now translating.

Again credit for the great growth of God's church in many lands must be given to the power of His *understood* Word and the Holy Spirit. Hearts have been converted from headhunters to brothers and sisters in the realization and love of Christ. Hate has been exchanged for compassion. Mental wretchedness has been replaced by peace of mind. Witch doctors have lost out to certified physicians. The love of God in Christ has overruled the people's fear of demons and Satan, filling their lives instead with unspeakable joy and glory.

Though the work of Slocum and Gerdel is most commendable, there are many other Wycliffe missionaries who are doing equally praiseworthy work.

God docs not want any to perish in hell, so we are commanded to go into all nations and preach the gospel (Matthew 28:18-20). And the first way of doing this is giving them the Word in their own language.

It grieves me to know of one who spends four years in college, then after two or three years in literacy training to become a translator, and even still falls through our fingers. Such a loss is due to lack of support or his not being assigned to a place of service. Yet we are told that the demand for translators is overwhelming.

Others are sent to the field, only to be assigned other duties, due to a shortage of support workers. The translators are trained to the equivalent of a physician or minister, yet they are doing tasks other than translating. This should never happen! We need a lot more support workers. Even Jesus said to His disciples, "The harvest is plentiful but the workers are few. Ask the Lord of the harvest, therefore, to send out workers into his harvest field" (Matthew 9:37-38).

In football every player supports and protects the ball carrier. If all the team members had the attitude of "What do we care about moving the ball and winning the game; we'll get our pay anyhow," that team would never achieve a victory.

The same principle is true in Bible translating. The goal is to translate the Word into every language, and the translators are carrying the ball. Certainly, they need and deserve every ounce of support possible. Let us never let one slip through our Christian fingers, no matter what, but support God's called workers in every way we can.

I believe translating the Scriptures is one of the greatest if not the greatest works one can do for the kingdom of God. I challenge each and all to find a Bible translator, then support that one consistently through financial assistance and prayer. I often think, "If I could suddenly find myself with a million dollars, I would start a fund of support for the translators, lest 'they get all dressed up with nowhere to go.'" It distresses me to see qualified specialists not being utilized in their God-ordained and vocationally trained ministry to eternity-bound souls. We need to work faithfully at this evangelistic opportunity before Jesus returns, at which time salvation opportunities will cease.

CHAPTER SEVEN
PRAYER'S POWER

Another tool Jesus taught us for a fulfilled life is prayer, which is a two-way communication with God. In prayer we pour out our hearts to Jesus and hear His direction. Evidence abounds that God hears–and answers–our prayers.

The subject is so important that instead of making it a part of the previous chapter on new life tools, we give this one (tool) a chapter all to itself, which it deserves.

September 28, 1993 I fell on concrete, shattering my left hip and breaking my left wrist. My doctor told me that the hip was all in little pieces, with nothing on which to pin or fasten an artificial joint. He advised letting it knit and heal first by itself so there would be something solid to which the socket could be fastened. He went on to say that there was only one chance in a hundred that all the pieces would interlace, but even if the hip did heal, arthritis would set in and a hip replacement would still be necessary.

My physician also said that the wrist was about the fifth worst out of 100 he had seen, but he did an excellent job, with God's help I'm sure. Though I was somewhat restricted in activity following surgery, I am now able to do everything with the wrist that I could before the injury. The truth is that I can even do more now because, before my fall, it was arthritic to the extent that I couldn't open my car door with it, but I can now because the arthritis is gone.

I was instructed by the doctor to use a walker until December 14, giving my hip some extra time to heal because of my age, 77. Admittedly, the hip was terribly sore, especially when I walked on it, so Christmas shopping was improbable. Then I yielded to the temptation of going deer hunting the first few days of January, which aggravated it and made it extra sore.

But a few days later, a marvelous (if not miraculous) thing happened. As I was walking out of the church house, Dick Rudman, a friend, asked, "How is your hip doing?" I replied that it was very sore.

He said, "Let me pray for you," and he did right there, as people passed by on each side of us. But God honored that prayer, giving me an almost perfect healing. There was a slight soreness, momentarily, when I removed my shoes and kicked them back under my chair later that evening, and there was another time of negligible pain when riding my bicycle a week later and tipped over. But now for more than four years I have felt absolutely no soreness in that hip. Our Lord does all things well! There is soreness in the other hip and many other parts of my body from time to time, but not in that hip. This convinces me that God answers prayer and that earnest prayer to God really works. In all honesty and fairness, however, I must also give credit to hundreds of Wycliffe people, my fellow church members, my family, and my friends, who were standing faithfully by in prayer during the entire time of my need.

Another example of prayer's power is illustrated by my son Eric and his family. They were in the Philippines, where Eric, a missionary pilot with JARRS (a part of Wycliffe Bible Translators) was flying translators and other missionaries in and out of their areas of service. Eric's mission was less than an hour's flight, which, on foot, was a two-day trip because of the lack of roads.

Having returned to the Philippines after a furlough, Eric and his family were living in staff housing because they did not have the finances to furnish their own housing, as is the case with most other Wycliffe missionaries. They were advised they would have to provide their own housing since the staff facilities were needed for staff personnel.

As they house-hunted, they found a house for sale for $5,000. Upon investigating, they learned, however, that another person already had his name on the buying list. Later, another house was available at the same price but was old and had termite damage. Through negotiating, the price was dropped to $4,000, but since they did not have even that kind of money, they took their need to the Lord in prayer. Within just a few days, a single donation earmarked for them arrived in the mail. A retired missionary couple had inherited some money, including a $4,000 bond which matured exactly at that time. As the retired missionaries prayed about how to use their unexpected gift, they decided, "We don't need this money (from the bond); let's give it to a missionary.

So they wrote down a few missionary names and began to pray. Soon they received their answer. The $4,000 should go to Eric and Carol Peterson! This was a miracle, an act of God at the precise time of need with the required purchase price of the house. Yes, prayer does change things by God Himself. He provides our needs, especially when we are doing His work. Jesus said, "But seek first his kingdom, and his righteousness, and all these things will be given to you as well" (Matthew 6:33). There are thousands of evidences that God answers prayer and that God's plan assuredly works.

In Luke 6:12 Jesus went to a mountainside and prayed literally all night. This praying without ceasing is a sure and true model for us to follow. Christ's main concern here was choosing His 12 apostles as we read in the following verse 13, "When morning came, he called his disciples to him and chose twelve of them whom he also designated apostles." These apostles were the key to Jesus' first mission to earth to live 33 years, then die to pay our sin debt.

Jesus spent all night talking the choice over with God. Some would say He prayed through or prayed until He knew God's answer. The choice was very important as these apostles were chosen to carry the gospel to the entire world, after Christ's ascension back to heaven.

Why the great soul-winning enterprise after Jesus left this earth? Because "The Lord is not slow in keeping his promise, as some understand slowness. He is patient with you, not wanting anyone to perish, but everyone to come to repentance" (2 Peter 3:9).

Since Christ Jesus, being the Son of God, had to pray all night, shouldn't we, being ordinary people, have to pray at least as much? We are commanded to pray without ceasing (1Thessalonians 5:17).

Again in Luke 18:1, Jesus said that people "should always pray and not give up," and at Gethsemane He told the Twelve, "Watch and pray so that you will not fall into temptation" (Matthew 26:41). Pray, pray.

Jesus promises, "But when you pray, go into your room, close the door and pray to your Father, who is unseen. Then your Father, who sees what is done in secret, will reward you" (Matthew 6:6). Jesus further promises to answer our prayers when we pray in faith: "If you have faith as small as a seed, you can say to this mountain, 'Move from here to there' and it will move. Nothing will be impossible for you" (Matthew 17:20).

To say "I can't be a Christian because I can't preach, teach, or sing; all I can do is pray" can be compared with saying, "I can't join the army because I don't have a rifle, or a cannon, or a fighter plane. All I have is the atomic bomb!" Never belittle a sincere prayer to God Almighty. God and one are a majority. Pray especially for your enemies. Jesus said, "But I tell you, 'Love your enemies and pray for those who persecute you, that you may be sons of your Father in heaven. He causes his sun to rise on the evil and the good, and sends rain on the righteous and the unrighteous" (Matthew 5:44-45).

Never forget that God isn't willing for any to perish in hell. In praying for our enemies, we have to forgive. It is not possible to continue hating someone you are praying for. Of course, the Lord knows this as well as He knows that unforgiveness hurts the one who was wronged more than the perpetrator of the wrong. But He wants us to learn that one great reward of prayer is that it changes the one who prays as often as it changes the circumstances prayed for.

I have prayed, as have many others, for Russia for more than 40 years, not necessarily that the Russians would embrace democracy, but that they would accept Christ and God's Word, the Bible. An additional object of these prayers has been that the Christians would not be persecuted beyond their ability to withstand. This tolerance has now come to pass, which so many thought would never happen. Even the Bible is being taught in Russian schools, and at this writing, Russia is still open to the gospel.

Christ's last command to the church should be our first concern. It bears repeating. He said, in Matthew 28:18-20: "Go and make disciples of all nations, baptizing them in the name of the Father and of the Son and of the Holy Spirit." In China the gospel spread more rapidly under the threats of communism, than it did through missionaries who preceded the communists. Therefore, if the road to heaven is paved with suffering, pain, ridicule, and humiliation, so be it! Life here, on the average, lasts 80 years. Life in heaven is eternal. And just think: we will be with Jesus and the family of God in a place unparalleled for its beauty.

The incredible suffering He would endure for the sins of the world were indelibly clear to the human Jesus, yet He did not flinch in His assignment. He was torn between His great love for us and His horrendous sacrifice and suffering on the cross. He loved us so much that He was willing to pay any price for us to enter heaven, yet He prayed to His Father that if there were any other way, "May this cup [of bitter suffering] be taken from me. Yet not as I will, but as you will" (Matthew 26:39).

The broader scene of this colossus is in Matthew 26:38-45: "Then he said to them, 'My soul is overwhelmed with sorrow to the point of death. Stay here and keep watch with me.' Going a little farther, he fell with his face to the ground and prayed, 'My Father, if it be possible may this cup be taken from me. Yet not as I will, but as you will.' Then he returned to his disciples and found them sleeping. 'Could you men not keep watch with me for one hour?' he asked Peter. 'Watch and pray so that you will not fall into temptation. The spirit is willing, but the body is weak.' He went away a second time and prayed, 'My Father, if it is not possible for this cup to be taken away unless I drink it, may your will be done.' When he came back, he again found them sleeping, because their eyes were heavy. So he left them and went away once more and prayed the third time, saying the same thing. Then he returned to the disciples and said unto them, 'Are you still sleeping and resting?

CHAPTER SEVEN

Look, the hour is near, and the Son of Man is betrayed into the hands of sinners. Rise, let us go! Here comes my betrayer!'"

When Christ said 'the spirit is willing,' in effect He was saying, "My love and compassion is for people to keep them out of hell and usher them into heaven. I truly do possess an enormous love for sinners, but I deeply dread all that intense suffering in this human body on the cross. The only way is for Me to pray through this. I need the power of prayer. I will pray till the answer comes."

Luke 22:43-46 describes more vividly the agony and deep concern of Jesus' prayer on the Mount of Olives. "An angel from heaven appeared to him and strengthened him. And being in anguish, he prayed more earnestly, and his sweat was like drops of blood falling to the ground. When he rose from prayer and went back to the disciples, he found them asleep, exhausted from sorrow. `Why are you sleeping,' He asked them. 'Get up and pray so that you will not fall into temptation.'"

It's obvious that the power of Christ's prayer gave Him strength and courage, even the comfort of angels, to lay down His life willingly so mankind could go to heaven. Yes, He suffered in our place without any degree of complaint, even to the point of praying to the Father, "Forgive them, for they do not know what they are doing" (Luke 23:34). What love! What compassion! What forgiveness! Finally Jesus gasped, "It is finished" (John 19:30), meaning, "Salvation's door is now open!" If we now accept Him into our heart, in true love, we are adopted into the family of God and inherit heaven for ever. This we will have a first fruit, as He had when He prayed His final earthly prayer, "Father, into your hands I commit my spirit. When he had said this, he breathed his last" (Luke 23:46).

I once read in *Guide Post* magazine of a girl from Pasadena, California, who was kidnaped by a would-be rapist and taken to a secluded place. But she began praying loudly, earnestly and unashamedly. Her bold witness of her faith in and connection with God so convicted her assailant that he backed off, accepted Christ as his Savior, sought counseling, and joined her church, the Lake Avenue Congregational Church. This report has been verified to me as truth by some of the congregation.

Never undervalue the available power of God through prayer. What the apostle Paul said in Philippians 4:13 is no fluke: "I can do everything through him [Christ] who gives me strength." But one must exercise this privilege in utmost sincerity and faith. You can never fool God. You can never outdo Him.

We now meditate on the high priestly prayer of Jesus, as recorded in John 17–a prayer for Himself, His disciples, and us.

But it is first necessary that we understand how Jesus prepares His disciples' hearts in love, compassion, and attitude for prayer in general. John 13-16 is an important prelude to the prayer of all prayers, preserved in John 17.

CHAPTER SEVEN

In John 13:1-12 Jesus gives an example of the humble servant by washing His disciple's feet, a service usually done by a slave. His act was then followed by an admonition: "You call me 'Teacher' and 'Lord,' and rightly so for that is what I am. Now that I , your Lord and Teacher, have washed your feet, you also should wash one another's feet. I have set you an example that you should do as I have done for you. I tell you the truth, no servant is greater than his master, nor is a messenger greater than the one who sent him. Now that you know these things, you will be blessed if you do them" (John 13:13-17).

This is another one of the great if not the greatest teaching examples in the matchless ministry of Jesus, especially in preparing us for his high priestly prayer of John 17.

Then He goes a step further in verses 34-35 of John 13 by saying, "A new command I give you. Love one another as I have loved you, so you must love one another. By this all men will know that you are my disciples, if you love one another. Therefore, we must have His kind of love if we are to pray meaningfully and understand the high priestly prayer of Christ.

Jesus continues instructing His apostles by saying, "Do not let your hearts be troubled. Trust in God, trust also in me" (John 14:1). Our belief and faith are very important factors in getting our prayers answered. Faith no larger than a mustard seed will move mountains. In John 14:6, Jesus answers a question from his disciple Thomas by saying, "I am the way and the truth and the life. No one comes to the Father except through me." Thus He declares His trustworthiness as the object of our prayers. He qualifies, He paid our debt, He was sinless, He fulfilled over 300 prophecies in his first coming to earth, and being of the Godhead, He has the authority to dictate the rules of truth and life.

One of those great truths is the power the believer has in prayer. Jesus said, I tell you the truth, anyone who has faith in me will do what I have been doing. He will do even greater things than these, because I am going to the Father. And I will do whatever you ask in my name, so that the Son may bring glory to the Father. You may ask me for anything in my name, and I will do it. If you love me, you will obey what I command. And I will ask the Father, and he will give you another Counselor to be with you forever–the Spirit of truth. The world cannot accept him, because it neither sees him or knows him. But you know him, for he lives with you and will be in you. I will not leave you as orphans; I will come to you" (John 14:12-18). What an enlargement for one's prayer life and understanding of Christ's high priestly prayer.

In John 14:23 Jesus continued, "If anyone loves me, he will obey my teaching. My Father will love him, and we will come to him and make our home with him." Again, in John 14:26 Jesus promises, "But the Counselor, the Holy Spirit, whom the Father will send in my name, will teach you all things and will remind you of everything I have said to you. Never underrate the power of the Holy Spirit; He is an ever present help in prayer. Jesus further prepared us for prayer by saying, "As the Father has loved me, so have I loved you. Now remain in my love" (John 15:9). Love is the key. And again Jesus promised, "I tell you, the truth, my Father will give you whatever you ask in my name. Until now you have not asked for anything in my name. Ask and you will receive, and your joy will be complete" (John 16:23-24). Even more power than we use is available from God. We are to ask for everything we need. Surely, this is awesome! How great God is! What a source of power we have through prayer in Jesus' name.

By now, Jesus had given His disciples enough training, using parables, so it was time to speak plainly. He told them, "Though I have been speaking figuratively, a time is coming when I will no longer use this kind of language, but will tell you plainly about my Father. In that day you will ask in my name. I am not saying that I will ask the Father on your behalf. No, the Father himself loves you because you have loved me and have believed that I came from God. I came from the Father and entered the world; now I am in the world and going back to the Father" (John 16:25-28).

Now Christ's teaching takes root and his disciples are sure of His meaning. Hear it in their own words, "Then Jesus' disciples said, 'Now you are speaking clearly and without figures of speech. Now we can see that you know all things and that you do not even need to have anyone ask you questions. This makes us believe that you came from God.'" (John 16:29-30).

The disciples thought that now they were solid as a rock, but Jesus gave extra help in a warning, "You believe at last!" Jesus answered. But a time is coming, and has come, when you will be scattered, each to his own home. You will leave me all alone. Yet I am not alone, for my Father is with me" (John 16:31-33). These words were spoken to give Jesus' disciples peace of mind during His upcoming crucifixion, lest they lose hope, and to ready them for what some call the high priestly prayer.

Remember that this prayer was first for Jesus, the second part for the disciples, and the third part for all of His followers down through the ages. It includes all 26 verses of John, Chapter 17.

Jesus prays for himself: "After Jesus said this, he looked toward heaven and prayed, 'Father, the time has come. Glorify you Son, that your Son may glorify you. For you granted him authority over all people that he might give eternal life to all those you have given him. Now this is eternal life: that they may know you, the only true God, and Jesus Christ, whom you have sent. I have brought you glory on earth by completing the work you gave me to do. And now, Father, glorify me in your presence with the glory I had with you before the world began.'"

Jesus prays for his disciples: "I have revealed you to those whom you gave me out of the world. They were yours; you gave them to me and they have obeyed your word. Now they know that everything you have given me comes from you. For I gave them the words you gave me and they accepted them. They knew with certainty that I came from you, and they believed that you sent me. I pray for them. I am not praying for the world, but for those you have given me, for they are yours. All I have is yours and all you have is mine. And glory has come to me through them. I will remain in the world no longer, but these are still in the world, and I am coming to you. Holy Father, protect them by the power of your name–the name you gave me–so that they may be one as we are one. While I was with them, I protected them and kept them safe by that name you gave me and none has been lost except the one doomed to destruction so that Scripture would be fulfilled. I am coming to you now, but I say these things while I am still in the world, so that they may have the full measure of my joy within them. I have given them your word and the world has hated them, for they are not of the world any more than I am of the world. My prayer is not that you take them out of the world but that you protect them from the evil one. They are not of the world, even as I am not of it. Sanctify them by the truth; your word is truth. As you sent me into the world, I have sent them into the world. For them I sanctify myself, that they too may be truly sanctified.

Jesus prays for all believers: "My prayer is not for them alone. I pray also for those who will believe in me through their message, that all of them may be one, Father, just as you are in me and I am in you. May they also be in us so that the world may believe that you have sent me. I have given them the glory that you gave me, that they may be one as we are one: I in them and you in me. May they be brought to complete unity to let the world know that you sent me and have loved them even as you have loved me. Father, I want those you have given me to be with me where I am, and to see the glory you have given me because you loved me even before the foundation of the world. Righteous Father, though the world does not know you, I know you, and they know that you have sent me. I have made you known to them, and will continue to make you known in order that the love you have for me may be in them and that I myself may be in them" (John 17:1-26).

What a prayer of love and understanding in the shadow of the cruel cross. It was only through Jesus' love that is beyond comprehension that He permitted and endured all of the crucifixion's agony. Agreeably, all of it is beyond our understanding. Prayer gave Him love and compassion to suffer it all to provide a way for us to be with Him in heaven with the family of God. It's no wonder that we sing at church, "I'm so glad I'm a part of the family of God; I've been washed in the fountain, cleansed by His blood. Joint heirs with Jesus as we travel this sod. I'm a part of the family, the family of God" ("The Family of God," by Bill and Gloria Gaither.) Since Jesus is within the believer, we believers should desire to be as close to God in our prayer life as Jesus was.

It is interesting to see how Jesus prepared His disciples for praying. Luke 11:1 says, "One day Jesus was praying in a certain place. When he finished, one of his disciples, said to him, 'Lord, teach us to pray, just as John taught his disciples.'" So our Lord's disciples, in their love and adoration, were eager to be enabled to pray in a God-pleasing way. So Jesus left them and us a model by which to go in our prayer life. It is called the "Model Prayer," or "The Lord's Prayer." [Some believe there is a distinction between the model prayer of Matthew 6:9-15 and the 26-verse prayer of Jesus in John 17, which they choose to call "The Lord's Prayer."] But regardless, the pattern of prayer given by Jesus is a striking one: "Our Father in heaven, hallowed be your name, your kingdom come, your will be done on earth as it is in heaven. Give us today our daily bread. Forgive us our debts, as we also have forgiven our debtors. And lead us not into temptation, but deliver us from the evil one" (Matthew 6:9-13). The King James version, as perhaps others do, makes "For thine is the kingdom, and the power, and the glory, for ever. Amen." the closing portion of the pattern prayer.

This awesome prayer basically covers all of our needs. Then Jesus goes further in helping us to have the right attitude for prayer–humility. "For if you forgive men when they sin against you, your heavenly Father will also forgive you. But if you do not forgive men their sins, your Father will not forgive your sins"(Matthew 6:14-15).

Then Jesus gives His followers more pertinent advise in Matthew 6:16-21. It reads: "When you fast, do not look somber as the hypocrites do, for they disfigure their faces to show men they are fasting. I tell you the truth, they have received their reward in full. But when you fast, put oil on your head and wash your face, so that it will not be obvious to men that you are fasting, but only to your Father, who is unseen; and your Father, who sees what is done in secret, will reward you. Do not store up for yourselves treasures on earth, where moth and rust destroy and thieves break in and steal. But store up for yourselves treasures in heaven, where moth and rust do not destroy, and where thieves do not break in and steal. For where your treasure is, there your heart will be also."

In this passage Jesus points out very clearly that the attitude of our heart must be right for prayer to be answered and we cannot be forgiven of our sins unless we totally forgive those who sin against us. Matthew 6:22-34 also talks about necessary attitudes for living in God's world victoriously, saturated in humble prayer. When we put God first in this world, He supplies our needs.

May we all search our hearts for a proper attitude and a consciousness of what we're saying when praying our Lord's prayer. Just reach out and touch Jesus in prayer. There is no word limit. The lines are always open. There is no long distance fee. He is waiting patiently for your call.

The number one agent in the child of God's arsenal is the privilege of prayer. And it is particularly important nowadays because of society's moral state worldwide. Moreover, when a church declines, it usually starts its decline by neglecting its prayer time.

It pleases me to see a church using Wednesday night entirely for enthusiastic prayer. In a reformed church I formerly attended, there was a five-minute period in each Sunday morning service. Such is not the case in the churches I now attend, and I miss that designated and regular prayer opportunity immensely.

CHAPTER SEVEN

Now is the time for us to devote ourselves to fervent prayer, especially on the National Day of Prayer (usually the first Thursday in May) because of the world's moral condition and need for revival. My prayer is that every church, mission, seminary, Bible school, Christian organization, and even secular groups across our nation will resort to a 24-hour prayer vigil. The ideal would be a World Day of Prayer from 8:00 a.m. Saturday to 8:00 a.m. Sunday, followed immediately by the Sunday morning worship service. The able-bodied could sign up ahead of time to pray at the church while the disabled could pledge to pray at a certain time at home. The idea would be to have a continuous 24-hour prayer vigil.

I'm told that the revival of the middle 1800s was immersed in fervent prayer in many churches and other organizations. Some even began with one person praying, then spread throughout the nation, and even into other countries.

James 5:16 admonishes us: "Confess your sins to each other and pray for each other so that you [our nation] may be healed." How true it is that the effectual, fervent prayer of a righteous man avails much. Oh, how our world needs a general healing. How desperately we need Christ's promised return to earth to heal our world's dilemma!

As is the practice of many others, my daily pattern of prayer is to start with Canada, then the U.S., Mexico, Haiti, Jamaica, Puerto Rica, Dominican Republic, Cuba, Granada, Central America, South America, Africa, Israel, Middle East, Europe, Russia, Mongolia, China, Japan, Nepal, Bangladesh, Burma, India, Southeast Asia, Philippines, Malaysia, Indonesia, Papua New Guinea, New Zealand, Australia, Madagascar, Sri Lanka, Solomon Islands, Fiji, and all missionaries and implicated missions. My main concentration is on Bible translation and printing prison/youth ministry, Bible distribution by radio, TV, and now Internet and satellite all from a world revival, humanitarian and economic standpoint.

I avoid political concerns as God's Word can work wonders in any governmental situation. But I do constantly pray for open doors to the gospel. I have prayed in this manner for years, and have seen numerous prayers answered, many of which were prophesied in the Bible and I believe, have been fulfilled.

May the worldwide church seek God in earnest prayer. We know that He has promised, in response, to heal our world. Prayer warriors, not just volunteers, are needed, such as 2.5 million youth gathering around their flag pole in fervent prayer. They are our future. But may we all participate because the whole world is involved. May we all take part.

Let us begin our day in prayer to God, who is waiting and listening, so that this loving and all-knowing great God of the universe may be with us throughout the day. Such will be a joyful experience.

Stop! Think! All existence points to His incredible great and incredible greatness, His super creation, His love,

CHAPTER SEVEN

His salvation in Christ, His fabulous heaven, His prayer-answering service, and even the horrible hell prepared for the devil, his angels, and followers. Truly, God is awesome. I surely want to be on His side, no matter what.

God's children know they should pray, but how and for what? A good order of prayer, accepted by most preachers and theologians is: adoration, thanksgiving, confession, intercession, then praying for personally known persons, the nation, world problems, and revival.

Jesus, in teaching the Lord's Prayer (Matthew 6:9-13, KJV) begins: "Our Father which art in heaven, Hallowed be thy name." He then puts adoration into obedient action by advising, "Thy kingdom come. Thy will be done in earth, as it is in heaven."

Since Jesus put adoration first in the prayer pattern, should we do differently? All 150 psalms are mostly devoted to adoration and praise, a fundamental part of worship. Jesus even ended His model prayer in adoration by saying, "For thine is the kingdom, and the power, and the glory, for ever. Amen." Adoration demonstrates our love for God, which assures Him that He can trust and fellowship with us for all eternity in heaven. So we lovingly beseech Him, remembering His unlimited love for us.

In our praying, we must never forget God's beautiful creation, which our God-given eyes behold. The loveliness of flowers astound our imagination, while many birds are like flying and singing flowers and fish allow us a scene unparalleled. What a topic for a poem or song! For many years I was in a formal church, where, even though we sang the praise and adoration hymns, the individual vocal expression of such was just understood and not practiced. We did have a regular five-minute prayer period, which I appreciated, and miss very much in the churches where I have worshiped since.

Upon retiring, I traveled often, worshiping in churches of all sorts, a goodly number of which spent much time in vocally adoring, praising, and giving thanks to God. In fact, one Sunday this lasted so long, no time was left for the sermon. The praise service was all done in an attitude of prayer, love, and lifting hands heavenward to God, which He blessed. Surely, much of our heavenly existence will be spent in like manner, so we should get accustomed to it while here on earth.

Later, while a member of a Dallas [Texas] church for 12 years, a prayer and praise time was observed at the beginning of the service. I needed and adored this special time. I felt that the Lord God was there and that I was a part of his kingdom.

At the church I now attend, we sing all of my childhood favorites, which I consider a treasured taste of heaven. Also, our Wednesday evening service consists mostly of prayer to God, which I believe more churches should do.

I look forward each week to this time of joy and excitement in thanking and praising God for His suffering for us, His forgiving our sins, His saving our souls, and providing all our earthly needs.

Confession and repentance are cardinal principles of salvation. Sometimes it's hard for those who grew up in the church to realize they are sinners along with everyone else, and recognize they need to repent and accept Jesus as their Savior. This ignorance reveals one of two things, if not both: Either their church is not emphasizing the new birth (John 3:1-21), or they are not listening.

An appalled preacher friend of mine says that he has heard three adult church members say, at different times, "When did I become a Christian? Why, I've always been a Christian!" That is neither what the Bible teaches nor what Sunday School teachers and pastors should be teaching and preaching. We were born sinners, and when the Lord begins to convict us of that condition through teaching and preaching, we must repent (have a born-again experience with God through Christ, confirmed by the Holy Spirit coming to dwell in our hearts). Jesus said it explicitly, "Unless you repent, you too will all perish" (Luke 13:3).

Correspondingly, we Christians can get to feeling quite self-righteous at times, yet we never progress beyond needing to confess our sins (for all Christians sin) to God in prayer. Such an act means taking an inward inventory: "Am I living in God's will? Am I becoming more like the Master? Am I pleasing Him in thought, word, and deed?" This type of action on our part is not done by compulsion, but by our free will from a heart that is appreciative and loving. One of my former pastors led us to confess our sins and rededicate ourselves to God twice a year.

Even Jesus commanded, "'Love the Lord your God with all your heart and with all your soul and with all your mind. This is the first and greatest commandment. And the second is like it:'Love your neighbor as yourself.' All the Law and the Prophets hang on these two commandments."

On another occasion Jesus was confronted by a lawyer, an expert in Jewish law, who quoted this same principle, but added "with all your strength" (Luke 10:27). Jesus replied, "You have answered correctly . . . . Do this and you will live [in heaven]."

We're all familiar with the expression, "An honest confession is good for the soul," which is indeed applicable to Romans 10:10. This verse says, "For it is with your heart that you believe and are justified, and it is with your mouth that you confess and are saved."

As loving God wholeheartedly makes us more aware of disobeying His will, so does our awareness of His awesome righteousness and glory becomes real. We can't make excuses and fool God. He knows everything and how each occurrence came about. He shows no favoritism of any kind. He thoroughly knows us, even to the number of hairs on our head. Since He is everything good personified, we should pray daily, "More like the Master I would ever be." 1 John 1:9 promises, "If we confess our sins, He is faithful and just and will forgive us our sins and purify us from all unrighteousness." What an awesome, loving, and forgiving God we serve! He paid our sin penalty, so our forgiveness is solely through Him. Let us make constant use of our prayer closet in confession and forsaking our sins, making prayer our first choice, not our last chance.

It is now time for intercessory prayer for the hungry, thirsty, naked, sick, lost, and imprisoned. Jesus said that ministering to these in prayer and action was the same as doing it to Him personally. "The King will reply, 'I tell you the truth, whatever you did for one of the least of these brothers of mine, you did it for me" (Matthew 25:40). What an honor He bestows on us in allowing us to minister to Him through others.

In Luke 6:27-29 Jesus commanded, "Love your enemies, do good to those who hate you, bless those who curse you, pray for those who mistreat you. If someone strikes you on one cheek, turn to him the other also. If someone takes your cloak, do not stop him from taking your tunic." So why worry about other's tricks on you! Be a prayer saint and pray for them.

Hear again Romans 12:19-21. Paul, inspired by God, wrote, "Do not take revenge, my friends, but leave room for God's wrath, for it is written; 'It is mine to avenge; I will repay,' says the Lord. On the contrary: 'If your enemy is hungry, feed him; if he is thirsty, give him something to drink. In doing this, you will heap burning coals on his head. Do not be overcome by evil, but overcome evil with good.'" So we are to pray for those who smite us because they desperately need assistance.

Submit the matter to Jesus in sincere prayer, realizing repentance is your adversary's problem, not yours.

As I pray around the world–country by country–I begin by praying that everyone worldwide will be able to hear or read the Word of God in his area by radio, television, Internet, satellite station, Far East Broadcast, Trans World Radio, shortwave radio, or Bible translation in his native language. I pray for Bibles for everyone, Billy Graham Evangelistic Association, hunger programs, Every Home for Christ, Campus Crusade, the Trinity Broadcasting Network, and many of the other validated mission ministries.

I pray especially for the fulfillment of Jesus' own prophecy in Matthew 24:14, "And this gospel of the kingdom will be preached in the whole world as a testimony to all nations; and then the end will come." I pray that everyone will know the sureness of God's greatness and that He created and controls the entire universe and all the natural and living habitat. I also pray that all may know the tremendous love Jesus has bestowed on mankind in voluntarily leaving beautiful and perfect heaven to save us from hell by suffering on the cross to pay the penalty for our sins.

Let us pray that everyone will take advantage of God's only plan of eternal salvation, that is, repenting and accepting Christ as his or her personal Savior, thus bringing about a great worldwide revival.

Pray that all may know that Jesus Christ is the only one who fulfilled all of the 300 plus prophecies in the Bible about the promised Messiah. All the others combined fulfilled only one prophecy, that of Matthew 24:24: "For false Christs, and false prophets will appear and perform great signs and miracles to deceive even the elect–if that were possible." But remember God said, "You shall have no other gods before me" (Deuteronomy 5:7), and be careful whom you follow.

Pray that everyone will know John 14:6: "Jesus answered, [Thomas] 'I am the way and the truth and the life. No one comes to the Father except through me.'" Know that Jesus is the proven answer to all the world's problems. All other plans are unproven theories that do not work.

Pray that in every country Satan will be bound, that prospective missionaries will be issued visas, that the doors for gospel ministry will open, that a great hunger for God's truth will arise and prevail, and that harmony and cooperation may be found among all missionary organizations since Satan and his demons always try to inject trouble. Also pray that each country will live the truth of Matthew 6:33: "But seek first his kingdom and his righteousness, and all these things [food, drink, clothing] will be given you as well."

Pray that each country will start its own Bible translating organization and send out translators so that the 3,000 language groups now without the Bible in their native tongue may see that sad predicament erased and that each country will print enough Bibles to permit every home in the world to own one. Pray for the missionaries in each country with their special problems, like the woman translator in Peru, whose translating partner died of cancer, leaving her to handle the challenge alone, despite her having cancer herself. God bless her.

Another translator stayed at the task rather than seeking medical treatment and died from his malady. These translating missionaries are a special breed and will have a very special mansion in heaven prepared for them. Yes, pray for them–their finances, health, acceptance, travel safety, and all their special needs.

These missionaries have hearts of gold and a great passion to tell others about their Jesus. They are far away from family and friends, even sometimes in hostile areas; so pray earnestly for them. They need help from a God who is willing to answer our prayers for them, supplying their needs. Never undervalue the power of prayer to God. Be a prayer partner.

Do not forget that there are 3,000 languages in our world that need a Bible translation. Presently they cannot read or know the riches of the Word because they have no word to read for that information. One thousand additional translators could be placed right now by Wycliffe Bible Translators alone if the translators were available. Also, many more support workers are needed. Is God calling you to this commitment? I encourage every other mission enterprise to assist the translating missions because getting God's Word into every language on earth is an urgent need! When a translating missionary works for a term of, say, four years with a people, giving them the truth of the Word in their heart language and gaining converts, they will remain true to the Word. But if not given the written Word, they will gradually mix in all their former idol worship while the missionary is on furlough, and upon his/her return, they will be far from the true worship of God. The true, unadulterated Word of God in their own dialect will keep language groups pure, if they are honest in their interpretation of it. Furthermore, it will also motivate them to evangelize, start new churches, and have revival on their own..

Pray for the hungry, homeless, and orphans around the world, especially homelessness and poverty in the Philippines; the flooded in Bangladesh; Satanism through Hinduism's reincarnation theory and the caste system in India; the war-torn in Yugoslavia, Rwanda, Somalia, and Zaire; the drought-stricken in Chad and Ethiopia; anti-Christian persecutions in Sudan; poverty in Haiti, Jamaica, Honduras, and Mexico; earthquakes in Iran; and catastrophe victims everywhere.

Pray for your pastor, Sunday School teacher, church and her spiritual quality, the unconverted, the ailing; for revival, community concerns, your family and friends. Remember, the prayer of a righteous person achieves much, and prayer changes things. Therefore, pray, believing God is awaiting your petitions.

Probably the most dire need of prayer is for the almost complete deterioration of our society, government, schools, entertainment, family, and environment. Let us not forget to pray for our president, his cabinet, our judges and lawmakers. Yes, when a church goes under, it usually begins with her prayer life, and I believe the same can be said of a nation. So please remain faithful in prayer.

Oh, how urgent is our country's need for Christian families! We must stay on fire (for God and Christian principles) in a cold (spiritually and morally), indifferent nation and world. We must reach out and touch Jesus in prayer. There's no limit to what can be accomplished.

I did not write these words on prayer because I think I'm an expert on the subject, but because of its importance, especially now in these days of rampant sin and corruption. Can we afford to sit idly by as the world of our day plunges toward paganism!

I know that prayer works and is the only answer to our world (spiritually and morally) as it hangs on the horns of a dilemma. God yearns for our prayers, and He hears them, meaning that a lot more earnest prayers are needed. Even when the economy looks good, fostering a feeling of self-sufficiency, do not forget that pride precedes a fall. It is later than you think. So pray individually and jointly, remembering that Christ is in the midst of two or three who gather in His name.

Fast and pray. The Bible teaches these two disciplines in no uncertain terms. I agree that these have been ignored by the present generation, placing in their stead feasting and palavering, but even that does not remove them from the Bible. Fasting should be done in an attitude of prayer. Moses prayed 40 days and Jesus prayed all night (Luke 6:12-13). The great need **now** is one alone with Christ. He can and will "reverse the curse." Our Lord can turn everything around. Let us pray, "Lord, take my life and let it be consecrated to Thee."

CHAPTER EIGHT
SALVATION'S PLAN

We have thought about the sureness of God, heaven, hell, the Bible, the soul (spirit), and God's creation. Now it's time to consider the key to salvation in Jesus Christ our Lord which gets us into the incomparable heaven. In this quest we will study the plan of God in a step by step pattern to lead a person to salvation in our Lord. Putting the subject of obtaining the new-birth status in our own words, we will examine the process in detail, using it as an outline for our text. This will entail, in some cases, the repetition of statements already made.

God, the creator, formulated the Law of Gravity in order to hold us to the earth. We cannot say that we're going to defy that law by walking off a tall building, because if we do that we will fall, possibly to our death. But far more important than gravity's law, are God's spiritual decrees of finding and knowing Him. Satan, originally an angel of high regard, defied these laws, for which he was expelled from heaven by God (Isaiah 14:12, Ezekiel 28:12-17). God's love includes you for here and eternity. He is a just and loving God, not desiring that anyone should go to hell, shown by John 3:16: "For God so loved the world that he gave his one and only Son, that whosoever believes in him shall not perish but have eternal life."

An even more meaningful way to say it would be: "God so loved (your name) that he gave his one and only Son, on the cross, to pay (your name)'s debt in a suffering of love, so that, if (your name) believes in him to the extent that (your name) stakes his/her life on him and loves Jesus in appreciation for suffering in his/her place, then (your name) shall not perish in hell, but shall have eternal life in heaven with Jesus."

Now for the full extent of that love, may I emphasize again that God does not want anyone to go to hell. That is why He sent His Son, Jesus, to suffer death on the cross in our place to pay the penalty for our sins. Sin has to be paid for, in a spiritual sense, just like our sins in the flesh do. Whether we like to admit it or not, there are penalties for crime, sexual promiscuity, acts of hatred, cheating, etc. Some of these penalties are prison, venereal diseases, execution, fines, lawsuits, living with a guilty conscience, and the fear of going to hell.

But Jesus loved us so much that He made the ultimate sacrifice in leaving heaven and its bliss, which He did not have to do, to come to earth, not in pomp but in humility. He was born as a baby in an animal stable, using an animal's trough for a bed, because people did not make room for Him in a decent place, that is, the only Inn in Bethlehem. Then before He reached the age of two, He had to be whisked away to Egypt, lest His life be ended by a jealous and wicked King Herod of Jerusalem. Even though Jesus actually was no threat to Herod, the spiritless monarch did not understand that. Therefore, he ordered the death of every child in Bethlehem two years of age and under in an effort to terminate the life of his thought-to-be rival. But through the foreknowledge of God and the obedience of Jesus' earthly father, Joseph, Christ was safely in Egypt during the massacre.

At the age of 12, Jesus accompanied Joseph and Mary to Jerusalem (from Nazareth His home) for the week-long observance of the annual Feast of the Passover, which celebrated the Israelites' exodus from Egypt in the long ago. On the return trip, after a day's journey, Jesus' parents could not find Him in the crowd of people with whom they were traveling. Luke 2:46-49 picks up the account: "After three days they found him in the temple courts, sitting among the teachers, listening to them and asking them questions. Everyone who heard him was amazed at his understanding and his answers. When His parents saw him, they were astonished. His mother said to him, 'Son, why have you treated us like this? Your father and I have been anxiously searching for you.' 'Why were you searching for me,' he asked. 'Didn't you know I had to be in my Father's house?" In verse 52 of the same passage: "And Jesus grew in wisdom and stature, and in favor with God and men." And as He grew, He labored as a carpenter until He was 30, at which time He began His public ministry. He, the true Son of God, received an humble baptism at the hands of John the Baptist. I find His being the Son of God, but yet receiving baptism from a mere man, as some sort of role model for us.

Our Lord, as a man, was tempted as we are. A good example of such involves His being tested as He began His public. The account is related in Luke 4:1-12: "Jesus, full of the Holy Spirit, returned from the Jordan [where He had just been baptized] and was led by the Spirit in the desert, where for forty days he was tempted by the devil. He ate nothing during those days, and at the end of them, he was hungry. The devil said to him, 'If you are the Son of God, tell this stone to become bread.' Jesus answered, 'It is written: man does not live on bread alone.' The devil led him up to a high place and showed him in an instant all the kingdoms of the world. And he said to him, 'I will give you all their authority and splendor, for it has been given to me, and I can give it to anyone I want to. So if you worship me, it will all be yours.' Jesus answered, 'It is written: Worship the Lord your God and serve him only.' The devil led him to Jerusalem and had him stand on the highest point of the temple. 'If you are the son of God, . . . throw yourself down from here. For it is written: He will command his angels concerning you to guard you carefully; they will lift you up in their hands, so that you will not strike your foot against a stone.' Jesus answered, 'It says: 'Do not put the Lord your God to the test.'"

Notice how Satan used Scripture to tempt Jesus. It is important to know that Jesus was sorely tempted by the devil under adverse conditions as we are, yet our Lord did not yield to temptation. This is another proof of His sinlessness and worthiness to pay the penalty for our sins. Since He was tempted as we are, He thoroughly understands our situation as human beings. His great love for us propelled Jesus to give up His life, thus providing a way we could be with Him eternally in heaven. Our part is to love and accept Him unreservedly into our hearts, letting Him live through us.

All through Jesus' earthly ministry, he was discredited and reviled by the religious scribes and Pharisees, and at one point even many of his disciples [not the Twelve] turned back and no longer followed him" (John 6: 66). Despite this and a host of other mistreatments, Jesus, in His great love and compassion, healed the sick, fed the hungry multitudes (5,000 one time, 4,000 on another occasion), raised Lazarus and others from death to life, restored sight to the blind, cast out demons, had no place to lay His head, and, without rest, performed miracles. His prayer life was regular and wonderful, even praying all night (Luke 6:12).

He unceasingly taught outstanding lessons–recorded in the four gospels–fitting **every** phase of life. What an inspiration it is to regularly read of his ministry. I am repeatedly amazed at His wisdom, due–of course–to His being a part of the Holy Trinity, which is to say, Father, Son, Holy Spirit. He was and is the God-man. He was and is the Savior.

But after an earthly life lived for others, Jesus was betrayed by one of his disciples, Judas Iscariot, into the hands of the scribes and Pharisees, who arrested Him. Our Christ was tried as a criminal, falsely accused, and unlawfully tried in a court, whose officials were persuaded only by riotous hollering. Pilate, the Judean governor (procurator), announced three times that he found no fault in Jesus. For this opinion, Pilate was accused by the maddening crowd of being no friend of Ceasar (an unfair sort of blackmail).

Our Lord was sentenced in the place of Barabbus, a fitting symbol of sin at its worst, being a seditionist and murderer (Luke 23:19). Jesus was spit on and punched in the face. His beard was pulled out, and a crown of thorns was thrust down upon His head in mockery. Then He was scourged by Roman soldiers and forced to carry His own instrument of death (the cross) until His strength failed Him.

After all this, He was literally nailed through both hands and feet to His cross, positioned between two thieves and identified in character with them. Hanging on the cross, just a smidgen from nakedness, Jesus was derided and given vinegar and gaul to drink. His side was pierced, and He was afterwards buried in a borrowed tomb.

And when He arose the third day as promised, His disciple Thomas and others were slow in believing it until they had personal proof. Then nothing could stop them from worship, praise, and witnessing about Jesus. They recognized Him as the sinless One who became a symbol of sin, died a substitutionary death, and paid the penalty for our sins in the most awful kind of death known at that time, fashioned by the Romans as the last word on suffering. Death by crucifixion was the nearest thing on earth to the torments of hell. The pain was unbearable, for if the prisoner relaxed, his breath was shut off, and if he raised up, the pressure on the nails was excruciating. But it was matchless love, not nails, that held Jesus on the cross. But, dear friend, you will experience that type of pain, even worse, in hell if you do not stop, seek God, and receive Christ into your heart.

Christ went through this hell on earth willingly–and even ended His meritorious act by praying for those who were taking His life. Alas, how His immeasurable love draws us to Him to know Him now and in anticipating being with Him forever in heaven! Remember that He promised: "And if I go and prepare a place for you, I will come back and take you to be with me that you also may be where I am" (John 14:3).

God's plan, as spoken by Christ was and is, "I have come that they may have life, and have it to the full" (John 10:20). The abundant life is not one of slavery to dope addiction, booze, rape, adultery, fornication, pornography, homosexuality, greed, or hate. Then why do those living such a life of degradation continue it?

We will live without sin in heaven with God, but in our earthly life we fall far short. This is because all of us "have sinned and fall short of the glory of God," as the book of Romans 3:23 declares.

Sometimes it's hard for clergymen's children, or those who grow up in the church, or good people to realize that they are sinners. Prisoners know this and are open

CHAPTER EIGHT

to the gospel. You and I have sinned. But God will forgive many sins as quickly as He will forgive a few. As an illustration, let's say that you committed every sin imaginable and that I only sinned once. You repent and pray, "Oh Lord, I'm an awful sinner. Please forgive me, as I will not do it anymore. This, Dear Lord, is because I love you for dying on the cross in my place." But I, on the other hand, reflect, "He ought to forgive me since I sinned only once." I would never be forgiven with that attitude, while you–in all of your many sins–would be forgiven because you truly repented.

So I'm not telling you to be good like me, because I'm a sinner like you. I only relay to you God's plan of forgiveness. Compare it to one beggar telling another beggar where he found bread to eat. We're all on the same level socially. My burden of concern is that you know about my Jesus in His saving power. He wants to have fellowship with you, but sin that is unconfessed and not repented of is keeping the two of you apart. Romans 6:23 says, "For the wages of sin is death, but the gift of God is eternal life in Christ Jesus our Lord."

When I was near the age two, our family had a beautiful collie dog, which I loved very much. I thought every dog in the world should look like that dog. In fact, I thought that other dogs were not real dogs. Barely tall enough to look over the window sill to see outside, I did so one day, just in time to see my dad shoot that dog on the last remaining layer of a haystack. The devastation upon my young mind of that scene, is perhaps why I remember it so well even now. I can still see–with my mind's eye–my father pull the empty shell out of the gun. I was too young at that time to understand the reason why that collie had to be killed. But when I got older it was all explained to me.

That well-trained cow dog would bring all the cows in from the pasture at a gentle walk–so it didn't affect the amount of milk they gave. If a cow didn't move or went in the wrong direction, this dog, not biting as most dogs would do under the circumstances, would throw all four feet against the cow, making her move where she was supposed to be. Reaching the barn, each cow was guided to her own stall; therefore, we had a near perfect canine, highly regarded by my father.

But a neighbor knocked on our door one day to apprize us of our dog killing his sheep. Dad couldn't believe the report and protested, "He can't be. He is locked in the barn all night, and he's with us all day." Still the neighbor insisted by saying, "I know your dog. No one in the community has a dog like yours, so watch him."

The next morning, the dog brought in the cows, and put them in their respective stalls. Then he lay in the barn window to watch the milking. But the minute the milkers began milking the cows, the dog was off to the neighbor's sheep pasture. Grabbing his gun, Dad went after him, about half a mile across the hills, and saw our dog standing with all four feet on a sheep, biting its neck. Upon seeing Dad, the dog didn't come to him, as was his custom, but went the opposite way in a big circle back to the house, where I witnessed his being shot. Father had no choice; he was compelled to kill the dog. You cannot live among people in a community where your dog destroys their sheep, even if the destroyer is a beloved pet. In like manner, God cannot run a universe, allowing those He cannot trust to be in heaven, as Matthew 7:21 confirms.

Our dog did almost everything right, as favors for my dad, not because he loved his owner and master, but to get favors for himself in return. Actually, that dog loved himself and did favors for himself in killing sheep.

In the same way, just doing favors (works) will not get one person into heaven with God. Such is like putting money in a Coke machine, expecting to get a Coke in return.

Only one qualified, sinless, God-man and promised Messiah, Jesus Christ, who in total love paid the penalty for our sins. He is our true Savior.

He Suffered for our Sins. God demonstrates His own love toward us, in that "while we were still sinners, Christ died for us" (Romans 5:8). He made a way which is an extra good reason for us to love and worship Him. While we were still sinners, He paid a debt He did not owe for our sake. And we owe a debt we cannot pay. So we can be in heaven with Him and His family if we accept Him personally.

He is Risen. Christ died for our sins. He was buried. He was raised on the third day according to the Scriptures. He appeared to Peter and then to the Twelve. After that, He appeared to more than five hundred (1 Corinthians 15:3-6).

And Jesus became the first fruits of our risen body. Proof of this for me is the story of Simon Greenleaf (1783-1853), the famous Royal professor of law at Harvard University. Greenleaf was a lawyer in the eastern United States, winning nearly all of his cases, so Harvard hired him to teach its young law students. He taught them to build a good case, getting all the evidence and obtaining all the facts.

One day a student asked him what he thought of Jesus Christ. Was He all He claimed to be? Did He really rise from the dead? Was Jesus truly the promised Messiah? Was He truly the Son of God and the Savior of the world?

The professor replied: "Oh, I don't think so."

The student asked, "Did you look at all the evidence?"

Greenleaf replied, "No."

The student continued, "Don't you think you should? You tell us to look at the evidence, get the facts, and find out the truth."

The professor replied, "All right, I will."

Several months later, Professor Greenleaf informed the class that he had checked it all out from every angle–history, Bible, archaeology, psychology–and came to the conclusion that the case for Jesus was the surest case ever and that it would win in any court of law. The professor added, "Jesus is the Son of God and all that

He claimed to be." Greenleaf became a devout child of God and wrote several superlative Christian books.

Being the quality lawyer Greenleaf was, you can rest assured that Jesus Christ truly is the promised Messiah, the Son of God. He did rise from the dead and is alive and with us today, listening attentively to our prayers and praises.

Almost everyone resorts to earnest prayer when in deep trouble and on their deathbed, definitely if he or she sees hell in an out-of-body experience.

Clarence Darrow, the famed agnostic lawyer of the Scopes trial in Tennessee, asked for three clergymen to pray for his salvation on his deathbed. When Dwight D. Eisenhower was near dying, he asked Billy Graham to come to his bedside and said, "Billy, please tell me again how to go to heaven.[10]

Charles Darwin returned to the Bible in his last days, being very sorry for his young life of uninformed ideas in connection with evolution and especially sorry for its taking such a hold on people. It seems that most people will read and believe anything that gives them a right to cling to their own pet sins.

The cross of Christ, which spiritually reaches from earth to heaven, reminds us of His great sacrificial love. If we appreciate and accept that love with a true reverent affection in our hearts and give ourselves to Him in true repentance, then God comes into our hearts. We do not

---

10. *Just As I Am by Billy Graham,* Harper Paperbacks, A Division of Harper Collins Publishers, 1997

rely on anything we do. We just completely accept Him, loving Him all the way–and that unashamedly.

My mother led me to the Lord when I was nine years old, assuring me that all I had to do was to repent, loving and accepting Jesus into my heart as my personal Savior and Lord.

I said to her, "Don't I have to prove myself for a while first?" She assured me that wasn't necessary, but if I loved and accepted Jesus and invited Him into my heart, He would help me. But she also said that if I really loved Him, I would seek to do His will.

So I took her word for it but wondered if God shouldn't make us prove ourselves first. This was despite the fact that I did have a real spiritual experience, even to the point of feeling called to be a minister.

Later I read of a man who went hunting with his dog and was shot. Two weeks later his body was found, with the dog standing faithfully by his side.

In another case, a man, a bear, and the man's dog were all found together dead. It was theorized that the man shot and wounded the bear, probably in self-defense. As the bear continued his attack, the dog tried to defend his master, but was cuffed and killed. Then the bear killed the man, but the bear died of his wounds. A dog, alone, can dodge a bear's cuffs, but in defending his master, this dog became an easy prey. What an object lesson this is in love and devotion, with no favors expected. The dog gave its life for its master.

CHAPTER EIGHT

Another story of a dog's loyalty to his owner tells of an older man becoming sick and his dog refusing to leave his bedside. When the gentlemen died, the dog followed the body to the cemetery and stayed by the grave day and night. Touched by the scene, neighbors brought food and water to the faithful animal.

But probably the best example of a dog being man's best friend is that of a retired man, whose dog had a litter of pups. Having lots of time, this man devoted full time to caring for and training the puppies. As a result, owner and pets became all but inseparable. One day the retiree noticed a strange look about the puppies' fur, and a veterinarian advised that they had an incurable mange disease, which would cause a painful death. On the advice of the vet, the master took his little friends to his pasture and shot them. Then as he stood there, lamenting his terrible loss, a wounded pup emerged from the brush and nestled itself between the sorrowing one's feet. The little one lovingly looked up at the man as if to say, "Though he slay me, yet will I trust in him" (Job 13:15).

These dog stories settled my mind on God's plan being right and workable. Even if He slays me, a beautiful and prepared heaven awaits me, which far exceeds anything on earth. We are winners either way, whether here or there, meaning that if we have the kind of love, represented by the examples just given, God comes down into our heart

Each person must accept Christ as Lord individually and personally in prayer with Christ Himself. When we die physically, we will meet Him spiritually, alone, one on one, answering for ourselves. We cannot excuse our behavior by claiming abuse as a child; we must rise above all excuses. His blood–and our acceptance of it–is the key to our entering heaven. "Whoever comes to me I will never drive away" (John 6:37). It is a sure promise.

Receiving Christ is God's Answer. "To all who received him, to those who believed in his name, he gave the right to become children of God" (John 1:12). *Children* does not mean kids, but refers to our being a part of God's family. Then we are heirs of the mansion in heaven Jesus has gone to prepare for us. Normally, when one is born of his parents, he is automatically part of that family, including being heir to a family inheritance. By the same token, *children of God* means being in the family of God, as well as inheriting heaven and eternal life. What a privilege to be in the family with Jesus, travel the golden streets, and behold immeasurable beauty forever.

"For it is by grace you have been saved, through faith and this not from yourselves, it is the gift of God–not by works, so that no one can boast" (Ephesians 2:8-9).

Here again we emphasize key words: *Grace, Faith,* and *Gift.* Let's first understand grace. Suppose you go to the police station to pay your speeding ticket, and five dollars is deducted from the fine. That's mercy. But if the ticket is completely torn up and the fine is canceled, that is grace. Psalm 103:12 expresses grace this way, "As far as the east is from the west, so far has he removed our transgressions [sins] from us." Our sins are completely forgotten, as far as God is concerned, if we are totally sincere about accepting Jesus.

Grace is a gift. It isn't "buy two and get one free," but it is entirely free, no cost at all. Christ Jesus paid all the price. We boast in Christ only, not ourselves. We give God all the credit. If we are wholly repentant and sincere in accepting Him as our Savior, we are entirely forgiven and are spotless in God's eyes. However, we often have to settle with society, especially if a prison sentence is being served.

We Must be Born Again in Our Spirit.. Hear John 3:3, 5-8 on the subject, "Jesus declared, 'I tell you the truth, no one can see the kingdom of God unless he is born again. . . . no one can enter the kingdom of God unless he is born of water and the spirit. Flesh gives birth to flesh, but the Spirit gives birth to spirit. You should not be surprised at my saying, 'You must be born again.' The wind blows wherever it pleases. You hear its sound, but you cannot tell where it comes from or where it is going. So it is with everyone born of the Spirit.'"

God Calls Us Personally. Jesus said, "I stand at the door and knock. If anyone hears my voice and opens the door, I will come in (to him)" (Revelation 3:20). This means opening the door of the heart (attitude, inner being) with the sure promise that Christ will enter. John 6:37 reminds us, "All that the Father gives me will come to me, and whoever comes to me I will not drive away."

Accepting Jesus Christ as our Savior and Lord means that we repent 180 degrees from self-control to inviting Him into our heart to control our lives and forgive us our sins by faith and trust.

Repentance is a most important word in obtaining salvation. One must repent of his sins. Both John the Baptist and Jesus taught that all must repent, that is, be sorry for their sins before God feel a great love and longing for Him, a love so strong that they turn from the sinful, selfish way of living to a life controlled by Christ's will. The repentance principle is strongly presented by John the Baptist in Matthew 3:1-2, "In those days John the Baptist came, preaching in the Desert of Judea and saying, 'Repent, for the kingdom of heaven is near.'"

Satan knows all of this (the above) better than we do because he is spirit, and he trembles. So just knowing isn't the answer. James 2:19 states, "Even demons believe that [that there is one God]–and shudder." Then verse 20: "You foolish man, do you want evidence that faith without deeds is useless?" The new birth comes to one's heart by a total surrender by the petitioner to Christ the Lord.

You can receive Christ at this very moment by faith through prayer (prayer is talking to God). And even talking audibly is not mandatory. God can and does read your mind (you inner intentions and attitudes). God is more concerned with the attitude of your heart, than He is with your spoken words. You can fool your mother, preacher, officer, judge, and possibly even a jury, but you cannot fool God. He reads your mind and plans.

CHAPTER EIGHT

Remember, Jesus left heaven for earth and died on the cross, voluntarily suffering in our place that we might become His child and a citizen of heaven. Don't let His unselfish and loving act be for naught in your life. If you are ready to accept Jesus as your Lord and Savior, you can pray a simple prayer, such as:

> Dear Lord Jesus: I need You! Thank You for dying on the cross for my sins. I open the door of my life and receive You as my Savior and Lord. Thank You for forgiving my sins and giving me eternal life. Take control of my life. Make me the kind of person You want me to be. Amen.

Congratulations! Should you die right now, you'd go to heaven and you are my brother in Christ–if you sincerely meant what you prayed. There's great rejoicing in heaven at this moment over you as a new convert to Christ. Jesus said, "I tell you, that in the same way there will be more rejoicing in heaven over one sinner who repents than over ninety-nine righteous persons who do not need to repent" (Luke 15:7). He continued, "In the same way, I tell you, there is rejoicing in the presence of the angels of God over one sinner who repents" (Luke 15:10). Praise the Lord. Give glory to His holy name! Thank the Lord often in your prayers.

Isn't there a song that has a title or contains words such as "When will people realize that people need the Lord?" The answer is that we need Him every moment in order to have a fulfilled life and our ticket to heaven. This is why we make Him our manager.

The promise of God's Word, the Bible (not our feelings) is our authority. The Christian lives by faith (trust) in the trustworthiness of God Himself and his Word. There is *fact* (God and His Word) and *faith* (our trust in God and His Word) and *feeling* (the result of our faith and obedience). John 14:21 says, "Whosoever has my commands and obeys them, he is the one who loves me. He who loves me will be loved by my Father, and I too will love him and show myself to him."

As Christians, we do not depend on feelings or emotions, but we place our faith (trust) in the reliability of God and the promises of His Word.

God's Word is wholly proven. Dr. J. O. Kinnaman, a respected scholar, declared, "Of the hundreds of thousands of artifacts found by archaeologists, not one has ever been discovered that contradicts or denies one word, phrase, clause, or sentence of the Bible but always confirms and verifies the facts of the Biblical record."[11]

The moment you received Christ by faith, as an act of your will, many things happened, including the following:

1. Jesus is settled within your being. Colossians 1:27: "To them God has chosen to make known among the gentiles the glorious riches of this mystery, which is Christ in you, the hope of glory." The obvious reality of Christ's life, values, image, virtues, thoughts, attitude and deeds

---

11. *The Signature of God, Grant Jeffery,* Page 70 and Frontier Research Publishers. Inc., July 1996

being in a Christian person is evidence that such a one is headed for glory (heaven).

2. Jesus forgave your sins. Ephesians 1:7: "In him we have redemption through his blood, the forgiveness of sins, in accordance with the riches of God's grace."

3. You are now a child in God's family. John 1:12: "Yet to all who received him, to those who believed in his name, he gave the right to become children of God."

4. Eternal life is your inheritance. John 5:24: "I tell you the truth, whoever hears my word and believes him who sent me has eternal life and will not be condemned; he has crossed over from death to life."

5. The quest for which you were born has started. 1 Thessalonians 5:16: "Be joyful always; pray continually; give thanks in all circumstances, for this is God's will for you in Christ Jesus."

Wow! What an opportune time to thank God for His sacrificial gift to you. God glories in your prayers and joyous appreciation. Your prayer is a most important part of salvation.

The Need to Develop Spiritually

Clearly no one is justified before God by the Law because the Bible teaches that the righteous will live by faith. Faith is the key word, which we can develop to the fullest degree by remembering that daily prayer is the will of Christ. "If you remain in me and my words remain in you, ask whatever you wish, and it will be given you" (John 15:7). Never forget the power and importance of prayer.

Precious to me is Luke 6:12: "One of those days Jesus went out to a mountainside to pray, and spent all night praying to God." Since Christ, being the Son of God, found it necessary to pray all night, shouldn't we, as ordinary people, pray at least as much? I Thessalonians 5:17-18 admonishes, "Pray continually; give thanks in all circumstances, for this is God's will for you in Christ."

Pray about everything–little or big–humbly and in faith all day long. Be constantly aware of the Lord God's presence every moment. Matthew 26:41 urges us, "Watch and pray, so that you will not fall into temptation." Such is good insurance to keep us from sin and to help us overcome temptation.

Enjoy God's holy word daily and learn by reading it. Acts 17:11 informs, "Now the Bereans were of more noble character than the Thessalonians for they received the message with great eagerness and examined the Scriptures every day to see if what Paul said was true. Daily Bible reading is a superb way to check out every sermon and find a spiritual church, remembering that much of the clergy is not preaching the true Word nowadays. Read full chapters, even entire books, of the Bible at one sitting.

CHAPTER EIGHT

This will enable you to understand all of it in context, getting the true meaning. Beginning with John's gospel; read it a few times first. Then read all of the four gospels (Matthew, Mark, Luke, John).

The Bible can be read all the way through in one year by reading three chapters per day through the week and five chapters on Sunday. However, sometimes–in certain parts of the Old Testament–the reading becomes a bit tedious, so I like the *One Year Bible* (or a similar plan) which lists a couple of chapters in the Old Testament with Scriptures pertaining to the history and prophecies about Christ's coming to earth, and some 20 verses of the New Testament that give Christ's direct teachings, miracles, and His life. Then the plan gives 15 verses from Psalms for prayer and praise, followed by a few verses from Proverbs for daily instruction.

I remind prisoners and retired people like me (I am 82), who have extra time, that about half of the New Testament (from Romans to Hebrews) was written by the apostle Paul, some five books of it while he was imprisoned. So those of us who have the time can spend it doing the greatest thing in the world, which is reading the Word and praying fervently. Ephesians 6:11 encourages us to "put on the full armor of God, so that you can against the devil's schemes." During His 40 days of temptation (Matthew 4:1-11), Jesus used scripture to withstand the devil.

Vow to be in loyal compliance with God's will. Jesus said, "Whoever has my commands and obeys them, he is the one who loves me. He who loves me will be loved by my Father, and I too will love him and show myself to him" (John 14:21). This promise makes it worth everything to obey God consistently.

Always show evidence of God's truth by word, thought, and deed. Jesus said to Andrew and Peter, who were fishing on the Sea of Galilee, "Come follow me, . . . and I will make you fishers of men" (Matthew 4:19). And to His disciples on the eve of His betrayal and arrest, He declared,"This is to my Father's glory, that you bear much fruit, showing yourselves to be my disciples" (John 15:8).

On this topic, the Great Commission excites and motivates me. "Then Jesus came to them [the 11 apostles awaiting His arrival at a mountain in Galilee] and said, 'All authority in heaven and in earth has been given to me. Therefore, go and make disciples of all nations, baptizing them in the name of the Father and of the Son and of the Holy Spirit, and teaching them to obey everything I have commanded you. And surely I am with you always, to the very end of the age" (Matthew 28:18-20).

We must remind ourselves daily that Jesus has commanded us to evangelize. Our Lord had a great passion for souls, which we should also have. Hear what 2 Peter 3:9 says about this: "The Lord is not slow in keeping his promise, as some understand slowness. He is patient with you, not wanting anyone to perish, but everyone to come to repentance."

We should allow nothing to stop us from spreading the good news of Christ's sacrifice. Paul was stoned and left for dead, but came up preaching the next day (Acts 14:19-21). He was happy to have suffered thus for Christ's sake.

Jesus was insistent about giving priority to preaching the gospel. He illustrated this in Luke 9:60, "Let the dead bury their own dead, but you go and proclaim the kingdom of God."

Again, He urges, "What I tell you in the dark, speak in the day light; what is whispered in your ear, proclaim from the roofs. Do not be afraid of those who kill the body but cannot kill the soul. Rather, be afraid of the One who can destroy both soul and body in hell" (Matthew 10:27-28).

Even the threat of death should not stop us from proclaiming the crucified Christ. If you cannot preach, at least help send someone who can and does. Hear Romans 10:15, 17: "And how can they preach unless they are sent? As it is written, 'How beautiful are the feet [the walk] of those who bring good news. . . .Consequently, faith comes from hearing the message and the message is heard through the word of Christ." God blesses those who excitedly witness for Him.

Allow true faith and dependence on God to be evident in every part of your life. Peter explains why we can trust God with our life, "Cast all your anxiety on him because he cares for you" (1 Peter 5:7). "Fear of man will prove to be a snare, but whoever trusts in the Lord is kept safe" (Proverbs 29:25). For one to be in God's will is for him or her to be in the safest possible place. 2

Corinthians 3:4 tells us "Such confidence as this is ours through Christ before God." Don't forget that God fed the Israelites each day for 40 years during the Exodus from Egypt to Canaan where there "isn't enough food for a sparrow."

And even Jesus fed the 5,000 and 4,000. These incidents have been verified by a recently found tablet written by Mark and buried in a cave in A.D. 68. This proves that we can trust His word in all things. Archaeologists have found nothing to disprove the Bible but have unearthed many artifacts to prove that His word is true.

Do not trust hearsay, but check it out. Be warned that Satan and his followers broadcast many half-truths which, in many cases give an exact opposite meaning from the truth.

Open heartedly honor God's Holy Spirit and let His power and influence reign in all of your life. Obey the Word in Galatians 5:16,17: "So I say, live by the Spirit, and you will not gratify the desires of the sinful nature. For the sinful nature desires what is contrary to the Spirit, and the Spirit what is contrary to the sinful nature. They are in conflict with each other, so that you do not do what you want." You are born again in the Spirit, so walk in Him, seeking God's will in everything you think, say, and do.

Jesus proclaimed, "But you will receive power when the Holy Spirit comes on you; and you will be my witnesses in Jerusalem, and in all Judea and Samaria, and to the ends of the earth" (Acts 1:8). The Holy Spirit gives one faith, confidence, authority, and power. Therefore, seek God's will and tell people about Jesus. Another cardinal requirement of Christian growth is forgiveness. You must forgive your adversary if you expect to be able to accept God's forgiveness. Matthew 6:14-15 teaches, "For if you forgive men when they sin against you, your heavenly Father will also forgive you. But if you do not forgive men their sins, your Father will not forgive your sins."

Forgiveness is of paramount importance to me as I work with prisoners, finding some who are filled with hate. Blaming someone else for their predicament. Some are possessed with a get-even attitude. Some say they cannot accept Christ yet because they have to settle a score first. I often wonder if they are saying they must commit murder to get even. But I tell them that the best way to get even is to forgive their enemies, for in doing so, they heap coals of fire on their heads.

Recently in Hondo, Texas, at the Joe Ney Unit, a prisoner who accepted Christ said this very thing happened to him. Years back in his hardened years, he approached a man who had wronged him to get even, but was met with a deep apology. The man asked him for forgiveness and this prisoner reported, "It blew my mind!" Romans 12:19-21 confirms this, "Do not take revenge, my friends, but leave room for God's wrath, for it is written: 'It is mine to avenge; I will repay,' says the Lord. On the contrary, if your enemy is hungry, feed him; if he is thirsty, give him something to drink. In doing this, you will heap burning coals on his head. Do not be overcome by evil, but overcome evil with good."

The Jesus way really makes sense. This is very important because you cannot be forgiven by God, unless you forgive all who have harmed you. Remember, He forgives us of our sins.

Since we all make mistakes, which are not always unintentional, we need forgiveness, necessitating our total forgiveness of those who have hurt us. Matthew 18:21-22 tells of Peter coming to Jesus with a forgiveness question: "Lord, how many times shall I forgive my brother when he sins against me? Up to seven times? Christ's answered, "I tell you not seven times, but seventy-seven times." [The publisher repeats that the King James Version, The Living Bible Paraphrased, and perhaps other translations understand Jesus to say we are to forgive seven times seventy, which would be 490 times, i.e. indefinitely.]

This is an astounding command, but Jesus left no doubt that He meant it, for He prayed, "Forgive us our debts, as we also have forgiven our debtors" (Matthew 6:12). Notice that here forgiveness is conditional. In effect we are saying, "Please forgive me *if* I, likewise, forgive completely." I believe this is a most important part of salvation, as well as a mandatory part of repentance.

Join a Bible Believing Church

Hebrews 10:25 instructs us: "Let us not give up meeting together as some are in the habit of doing, but let us encourage one another–and all the more as you see the Day approaching." Remember the Bereans, who searched the Scriptures daily to see for themselves whether what they had heard was true. Every word and statement of the Bible is true without one false claim, based on hundreds of thousands of artifacts collected. Jesus said, "For I tell you the truth, until heaven and earth disappear, not the smallest letter, not the least stroke of a pen, will by any means disappear until everything is accomplished. Anyone who breaks one of the least of these commandments and teaches others to do the same will be called least in the kingdom of heaven, but whoever practices and teaches these commands, will be called great in the kingdom of heaven" (Matthew 5:18-19).

These are very strong statements of Jesus, so don't ever compromise or minimize any part of God's holy Word. Especially since archaeology, history, and science support it as solid truth. Our God is an awesome God. His Word is true. Seek a church that preaches Biblical truth and worship (in spirit and in truth), develop spiritually and morally there, and serve our great and gracious God there.

The Little Gold Book

As mentioned earlier, I work as a counselor with the Bill Glass Ministries, Prison Ministry division. This work consists of going into prisons on weekends to minister to the spiritual needs of inmates. These ministering groups use a copyrighted booklet, titled *The Four Spiritual Laws,* by Dr. Bill Bright, founder of Campus Crusade for Christ. The four spiritual laws are basic to our subject and they guarantee that all counselors are teaching the same theology. Furthermore, they provide a good and easy outline for leading a person to Christ. Even a beginner–with a little training–can use them effectively.

After one has prayed to accept Christ, the *Four Spiritual Laws* booklet is given to that person. This enables and encourages the convert to use it in witnessing to loved ones and new inmates as they enter the prison. This approach proved very successful in an Oklahoma prison where practically all of the incoming prisoners had been led to the Lord upon our return a few years later. One new inmate said to me, "I arrived here yesterday, and two inmates have already approached me to receive Christ."

As a rule, I do not use all the extra instruction I have shared in this writing, but after explaining how to become a child of God, I will stop and ask, "Does this make sense to you?"

If the answer is hesitant or "no", then I give additional information. However, it is not necessary to add anything to the *Four Spiritual Laws* as they are quite complete and effective as they are.

When one of our special guest speakers gives an altar call, or if the time is short, or if the person has already decided to accept Christ, I usually begin my counseling with the prayer (on page 10 of the *Four Spiritual Laws* booklet).

In my prison work, I never knowingly alter the *Four Spiritual Laws* pamphlet in any way, but mainly use it

CHAPTER EIGHT

to bring about a deeper understanding of God's Word. I am referring to a deeper comprehension than is often obtained from other sources, such as general teaching of the Bible from the pulpit or Christian literature. My aim is especially to emphasize the awesome sureness and truth of the Bible, God, Christ, creation, heaven, hell, spirits, and God's Holy Spirit. Please consult the bibliography for additional source material.

CHAPTER NINE
IT'S ACTION TIME

We've discussed in this book what sure truth is, and what it is not. But just talking about it is like a rocking chair: one can get it going, but it doesn't take the occupant anywhere.

Accepted or not, we have much proven truth at our disposal, and should ignore the multiplicity of theories that have never been proved. Even though Charles Darwin (1809-1882) swept the world off its feet with his evolutionary theory, remember that he died with a Bible in his hand.[12]

Doubting Thomases have jeered at God and the Bible, insisting that when the missing link is found, their theory will be substantiated, but there is no missing link and never has been. Such contentions are of Satan. Birds are birds, fish are fish, and mammals are mammals with no in-between. They are today exactly as God Himself created them. Such is true for all species, including human beings, created by God in His own likeness. "So God created man in his own image, in the image of God created he him; male and female he created them" (Genesis 1:27). There are no evolving species. In fact, there are fewer species now than when they were first created, which is due to extinction. There are many ways of dating artifacts, some of which are quite reliable, but conveniently only the unreliable ones that fit the false theory of evolution are used.

In other words, a lie is used to cover a lie! When Jesus returns, as He has promised to do, the evolutionary theory will be scrapped; so why don't we do it now![13]

Don't risk the dreadful results of believing a lie; check it all out carefully, looking for the real truth. Read, study, pray! Give God the credit for this magnificent world's creation. Praise and thank Him for it all, and for His Son Jesus. Not to do so is doing God an alarming injustice. Rather, let us be like the person who received an anonymous and costly gift. Not knowing who the donor was, he was good to everyone he met, lest he miss being grateful to the giver.

I'd rather give God credit for this awesome universe and be wrong than to offend One so powerful, worthy, loving, and kind. In comparison with the indescribable universe God created, I am but as a dust particle in size. Consequently, whatever He says, I will believe and do, regardless of who my peers may be.

I have no desire to be on the side of a loser—and Satan is

12. *Voices From the Edge of Eternity*, by John Myers

13. The Institute for Creation Research, PO 2667, El Cajon, CA 92021

a loser. He definitely did not create one speck of the world. His role in life is to tear down and cause problems. Does it make sense to side with the world's greatest loser when we can be on the side of the world's greatest winner–God! If God be for us, who can stand against us. It's not a gamble, a chance, or an imagination of the mind. It is the only sure thing.

Our Sick Society

I believe people have enough sense to know things are going wrong morally in our society today. Then the only sensible conclusion regarding the moral condition of our present world is that it is deplorable. Our prisons are filled to capacity while convicted and sentenced lawbreakers wait in line. When and why did this degeneracy occur? It's a result of God, the Bible, the Ten Commandments, and prayer being removed from our schools and replaced with the devil and his evolutionary theory. Not only is such a move not working, it is fast moving us toward calamity.

The week these words are being written, a letter to the editor of a Texas weekly newspaper screamed, "May God Help Us! I was very disappointed when I read of the negative vote on allowing Bible history in our local schools. What ever happened to men who take a stand? What ever happened to men who put their faith in God above their political ambitions? I am concerned about our churches and their leadership and our public school system. It is sad to see Christian men behave like a bunch of wimps! May God help us; it seems that our politicians won't!" What was the motive in the terrible spiritual and moral change that has inundated our world since 1960? Mainly, it was to expel from the earth God and all His basic guidelines for noble living. Jesus said, "The thief comes only to steal and kill and destroy; I have come that they may have life, and have it to the full" (John 10:10). A careful and honest examination of the evidence undeniably proves that God, Jesus the Christ, the Bible, creation, heaven, and hell are valid. Actually, they are more credible than is the fact that you are reading these words.

We need a foxhole experience or a severe heart attack to wake us up! It has been said that there are no atheists in a foxhole or the hospital emergency room. Don't laugh; it could happen to you.

Most creation scientists were former evolutionists, but nothing in evolution made sense scientifically. They found, however, that everything fell into place scientifically in the creation doctrine. Most of the learned who remain in the evolution camp know better but stay put for political reasons or job security. Many school teachers endorse evolution for the same reason, but some switch to Christian schools at a lower salary rather than teach a lie. The theory of evolution must be put on the defensive. Evolution could not and did not happen.

I'm told that top evolutionists warn their people never to argue, debate, or go to court on the issue of evolution versus creation with a creationist because the creationist will win every time. I say it is time we took the issue to court, if for nothing else but to set the record straight. The 1925 Tennessee false trial that showed a wild pig's tooth as evidence of the missing link in man's evolvement from a monkey was a ridiculous sham. A retrial is needed. Are all the God-fearing Christians asleep?

We have the truth. God is on our side which makes us a majority, so we must bring about a complete stop to the moral insanity that's enveloped us. Many, especially our youth, are destroying their brains and lives with dope, AIDS, gang shootings and knifings, rape, unwed pregnancies, abortions, divorces, and murders. Many draw prison terms because of life styles born of obscene and salacious looking and reading. (It's commonly called pornography!)

Yes, we are putting a curse on our young people by allowing these illicit, smutty, dirty, lewd, foul, nasty, vile, unprintable, unspoken programs not only to exist, but to continue. Shame on us! Those who perpetrate such junk should serve prison sentences too as partners in crime. Jesus told us in Matthew 18:6 that drowning would be the least painful death for anyone who caused a "little one" to sin.

Jesus put strong blame where it belongs. Causing anyone to sin is the vilest of all sins in the mind of Jesus. The waywardness of our times has gone too far; the time has come to put a stop to it all. Let us earnestly pray, write letters, boycott Satan, warn your people (the future generation), and march–even to Washington, our country's Capital, if need be.

But absolutely and finally, the best answer to this dilemma is to lead our citizens and fellow human beings to a born-again experience in Christ. Today's world is in urgent need of revival. It's not enough to admit that God is real; He must be real in a person's heart. That realness gives total reverence, love, and obedience to the great God of this planet, to our Savior Jesus Christ, and to the Holy Spirit, who dwells inside the born-again child of God.

We must pray till the answer comes and carry out the worldwide command of Matthew 28:19 to teach all nations and baptize them as Christ's disciples. We need to be on fire, obsessed with telling others about our Jesus and His salvation for everyone who repents and accepts Him in love.

Christ admonished us to lay up for ourselves treasures in heaven, and people are the only things we can take to heaven. Billy Graham has been in nearly every country of the globe preaching or attempting to preach the gospel to "a lost and dying world." I believe that in heaven he will have showers of blessings. So will we if we repeat his example.

Christ is the Answer

In that town where the missionary saw everyone made born-again Christians and nobody in jail depicts a scene of heaven on earth. Christ in a person's heart is truly the answer to earthly heaven, instead of hell on earth.

Many young people, as well as older ones, are getting into serious trouble. As this book is being prepared, Arkansas is grieving over killings at school by mere children (boys). A similar tragedy happened in Oregon only a few days ago, when a 15-year-old boy killed at home, then on to his school to slaughter there. Parents are being disobeyed, disrespected, and even attacked by sons and daughters. We are now experiencing hell on earth, but the indwelt Christ can, will, and does turn the trend around. When Christ comes in, the hatred and desire to destroy disappear.

Yes, if everyone on earth became children of God by being born again, this would be a wonderful world in which to live, with life full and meaningful. Such is the reason for which Jesus said He came to earth (John 10:10). He stated plainly in John 15:11, "I have told you this so that my joy may be in you, and that your joy may be complete."

What an incentive for our doing everything possible to get God's Word out, using radio, TV, Internet, and the many other channels open to us. Even a Christian march on Washington is a possibility worth considering.

Are there, will there be counterfeits–fake Christians? Yes. Anything of value will always have counterfeits. But that truth doesn't make Christ any less the way, the truth, the life, and the answer. Be assured that all false Christians will be recognized, denounced and punished on Judgment Day. Yes, it's true that Christ and all genuine Christians suffer greatly because of the many phony Christians and fake Christs.

Giving toward printing Bibles is another excellent way to spread the Word. Our goal should be to get a Bible into the hands of every person in the world in his own language. Such is not impossible. Of course, many countries do not even have a written language, so a Bible translator must go in, and with the help of a native, learn the language, design an alphabet and dictionary, and then translate the New Testament.

These translators deserve a special place in our prayers and appreciation, as their ministry is a gigantic and strategic one. They must complete college first, literacy training next, then the missionary must be accepted by a mission. Upon acceptance, he/she must visit many churches seeking financial support for the work. How regrettable that some never get the required support and fall by the wayside. I am praying that someone will start a fund support organization strictly for translators and literacy missionaries in order to utilize all whom God calls to this service. May each of us find a Bible translator to support, at least to some extent.

But prayer is our greatest tool in turning this whole matter around–and God knows we need an about-face. Jesus said that even a little faith could move mountains (Matthew 17:20). He also gave his disciples "power and authority over all devils, and power to cure diseases" (Luke 9:1). Satan is our problem, so let us pray earnestly that he be bound in the name of Jesus of Nazareth.

Now's a good time–in one accord–to organize 24-hour prayer vigils in every church and mission across the nation. May we *all* humble ourselves and pray, believing and without ceasing, till the answer comes. With Satan bound, let's pray for a great revival in our nation and world saying, "And let it begin in me." As we pray, let us vow before God that evolution is a hoax and a lie–that God and God alone–in love and goodwill created it all. Then He gave it to us. But that's not all: He gave us His Son, who gave His life for us on the cross, making our eternal salvation possible.

Pray that entertainment smut will be removed, that there will be a turning away from dope, that sex and violent crimes will cease, and that there will dawn a great and new awakening wherein people will forsake sin and place their lives in the hands of God.

Pray that our president, lawyers, courts, judges, and lawmakers will all look at the evidence honestly, and turn their lives over to our Lord and His will. It would return America to the fundamentals.

All of which we speak here must be carried out in God's love. Let us be doers of God's Word, and not hearers only. A top state prison official in Texas once said:

> "The worst trouble with our nation isn't primarily drugs, rape, alcohol, robberies, murder, gambling, and the like. The problem is in the 50 million Christians in this country who are afraid to witness outside their own group or church."

We need to turn the world upside down for Jesus.

CHAPTER TEN
<u>WE CAN DO IT!</u>

Through our entertainment industry and even in some of our schools, we, perhaps unconsciously, are poisoning the minds of our youth and teaching them conduct for which later we imprison them. That doesn't make sense, does it? Our youth are being trained to be the kind of people who are no longer safe to be around. The answer to this problem is prevention, that is, do not put such terrible thoughts in our youth's heads in the first place. Yes, an ounce of prevention is surely worth a pound of cure.

Another problem in present-day society in America is that we are living on borrowed money, leaving future generations a debt they can never liquidate. In fact, the problem has grown so big that only God can correct it through a nationwide revival, that is, a turning to Divine morals and principles that produce responsibleness in the handling of money. One thing is for sure, when Christ returns to earth, which is not long off, He will solve the problem. And He could come today. His first coming to earth was promised, and He came. His second coming to earth is promised in the Bible, and He will surely come. This Christ, of whom I speak, is a heart-changer. He changed three of the nation's worst criminals into respectable citizens, and He will change your heart too.

The Solution

What I believe needs to happen (and I long to see it) is for all evangelical and concerned Christians to unite in a week-long all-out campaign. This would include marching (in a peace-loving way) on Washington, a 24-hour prayer vigil, and a national or worldwide evangelistic crusade with a heavy youth emphasis.

This crusade would proclaim the certitude of God's being the author of creation and declaring the fallacy of the evolution theory. The crusade would also exalt God, Bible truth, Christ, salvation, and heaven. The campaign would likewise emphasize the prison ministry, prophecy, archaeology, true scientific data, the *Jesus Film*, the *Four Spiritual Laws*, our true Christian heritage, Bible translation, Promise Keepers, and the stopping of movie and television smut, wrongful sex, and hate.

The campaign would also plead with all people, the president, the lawmakers, lawyers, judges, and all leaders to forget their biases and honestly look at the evidence, then do only that which God condones. It is insensible to fight against God when we are as only a speck of dust in comparison with the earth or the solar system. And they are as a speck when compared with the whole universe. Never forget that our great God made and controls it all. Even the very hairs of our head are numbered.

I'd like this crusade to last at least a week with up to 10 million participating in the Washington march. It could possibly start with the National Day of Prayer, which is the first Thursday in May, or the beginning of that week with a 24-hour prayer vigil ending on Sunday, with all the churches having their own prayer vigils at the same time. Each hourly program would start or end with a five-minute prayer time. Every person, church, mission, and Christian organization would pray earnestly during that time.

This plan would include a worldwide evangelistic effort televised each day from 7:00 to 8:00 p.m., hopefully led by the Billy Graham Evangelistic Association—one hour per day, or preferably a whole day, dedicated totally to our youth in creating a genuine spiritual hunger among them.

Creation versus evolution should be given top priority with at least one hour of prime time in which undeniable evidence that God "created the heavens and the earth" would be presented in short, hard-hitting, easy-to-understand increments. How wonderful it would be if such an effort would send the whole creation controversy to court and reverse the false verdict of the Scopes trial in Dayton, Tennessee, in 1925. A creation scientist from either Glen Rose, Texas, or El Cajon, California, plus other archaeologists, could give convincing input.

CHAPTER TEN

The prison ministry is one of the most effective soul-winning ministries of today and the most life-changing. At least one or more hours should be used for this ministry, with Jack Murphy or Bill Glass from Bill Glass Ministries speaking.

The teaching on prophecy should be more on those prophecies fulfilled or proved than on the ones yet to be fulfilled. There are many good Bible prophecy specialists with positive evidence, who can deliver information without wasting time. Archaeology is also an important tool to prove the authenticity of it all. Let the rocks cry out. Science should not build its case on a bias, but always seek the truth from all experiments.

Christian heritage, especially in America, furnishes impressive evidence of how God works and blesses. Most people have been misinformed as to what transpired among our founding fathers, as they witnessed many miracles of God. Dr. D. James Kennedy is an able authority on this and back to basics, the solid principles of God and the Bible, on which our forefathers founded this nation.

Bible translation is a productive part of getting the Word out to the people of the world and should be given much air time. David Cummings, president of Wycliffe Bible Translators from Australia, is a very dynamic speaker for this time.

Promise Keepers is a timely part of our evangelism and quite an encouragement to a fulfilled Christian life. This organization should be given a day, depending on time

WE CAN DO IT! PAGE 209

available. At least one hour should be given to warn our youth about the dangers of moral smut and illicit sex.

Pertinent Facts

We've been talking about awesome truth of the greatest offer ever made about the greatest story ever told about the greatest man who ever lived who did the greatest deed ever done to pay the penalty for our every sin. And this awesome joy is dependent on Jesus.

The Bible is a book of prophecies and their fulfillment. It is filled with awesome truth and consequences. The Old and New Testaments are all about Jesus and His coming and His fulfilling all of between 300 and 456 clear prophecies concerning His first coming. It has 257 prophecies in reference to His second coming.

So His coming, and the end of the world could be today. Don't despair! His first coming was prophesied and He came; surely He will come again. You can count on it. His salvation is free for the asking. Just open up your heart.

These prophecies were all made by God Himself—400 to 1,400 years before Christ and up to 3,400 years ago for Christ's second coming. History is all falling into place. These fulfilled prophecies are all miracles, happening in the providence of God. They are not theories but proven truths.

Christ claimed to be God's Son and proved it. He gave His life for a people in great danger. Don't hide your head in the sand like the proverbial ostrich; check the facts out for yourself now–this very minute. The matter is too crucial to ignore. Jesus made a way! Our Lord is not willing for anyone to perish in hell. You will know the truth of the Bible for sure five minutes after you die, but then it will be too late to do anything about your calamity.

Jesus Christ rose from the grave for us and now lives for us. He whom the Son sets free is free indeed, even in prison. Read the postscript, "I am coming back." If you are alert, you'll not get hurt. With Jesus in your heart, you're always a winner, no matter what happens.

For Mary this was very true. She went to the house of Zechariah, a priest who could have had her stoned to death for being unmarried and pregnant if her pregnancy had not been of God. The fact that she lived is a positive sign of her virginity during pregnancy–absolute proof that Jesus was the true Son of God and our awesome Savior of the world.

All that happened in the Bible was in the plan and the providence of God, pointing toward the coming of our Lord Jesus Christ. Just think of all the awesome, miraculous, and wonderful things that He did in healing, raising the dead, feeding the hungry multitudes, causing the storm at sea to subside, walking on the water, and teaching the disciples and the masses. But that's not all He did. He suffered crucifixion–without complaint–to pay for our sins. He even prayed for His enemies. He rose from the dead and taught His loving followers even more about having a passion for lost souls (Matthew 28:

18-20). What awesome love Jesus revealed, not wanting any of us to perish in hell. And because of that, we should eagerly tell everyone about our loving Lord, who had and has an unimaginable passion for souls.

What a comfort in knowing that He is with us always, even Christ, who said, "All power is given me." That is the Christ within us–His redeemed–so we have all power through Him. It's not I, but Christ in me!

This Book

I pray that this book has given you the solid assurance of our awesome God, His Son, His Word, His love, His Holy Spirit, His creation, His heaven, and everything in His plan–a plan that included our salvation. Don't let your inheritance go to waste. Don't let all that our Lord has done for *you* down through the ages, especially His suffering in love on the cross for all mankind, be for naught in your life.

You have a choice: you can–through Christ–help effect a change in the world for good or you can help change the world for bad and for Satan. Which will it be? Heaven, I win! Hell, I lose!

There is much more evidence. The surface has only been scratched. Check out the resource list in the bibliography.

A Final Review

1. One to three million Israelites were fed by God during the Exodus, each day for 40 years in the

desert where there is hardly enough food for an ant and He supplied enough water for up to thee million people and their animals for 40 years, where there is practically no water at all.

2. A cloud provided protection from heat and cold and gave guidance 24 hours a day for 40 years.

3. God provided an impossible crossing of the Red Sea for the Israelites overnight during the Exodus.

4. A host of Israelites crossed the Jordan River–at flood stage–at the end of its 40-year journey to the promised land.

5. Some 2,000 prophecies made in the Old Testament were also fulfilled in the Old Testament.

6. More than 300 prophecies made during 1,400 years promising the coming of the Messiah were all fulfilled in the coming of our Lord Jesus Christ the first time.

7. Not even one of the prophecies pertaining to the first coming of Christ was fulfilled by anyone other that Christ Himself.

8. At least one of those prophecies denotes the very year of His ministry.

9. One of those prophecies reveals the city of the birth of Christ, which was named Bethlehem of

the county of Ephratah, not even a town at the time of the Old Testament prophecy.

10. Two hundred and fifty-seven prophecies exist about Christ's second coming, some of which deal with events that will precede his coming, and, I believe, have already been fulfilled. Christ is coming soon.

11. Fifteen historians–in addition to Josephus and Pontius Pilate–wrote during Jesus' time, and all wrote of Christ and His acts.[14]

12. Jesus, alone and only, paid the penalty for our sins, and He did it voluntarily in love, forgiving His accusers.

13. Hundreds of thousands of artifacts have been unearthed, with not one disproving but all in one accord corroborating Biblical claims.

14. The deterioration of the earth's magnetism could not have started more than 10,000 years ago, making the earth very young, too young for evolution to have possibly happened. The only sensible explanation is: God created it all!

15. In the area of Glen Rose, Texas were found dinosaur tracks, man's tracks, extinct tiger tracks, and several other fossil evidences believed to be extinct up to 500,000 years ago, by false Carbon 14 dating. All were found together in the same

---

14. *Why I Believe*, by Dr. D. James Kennedy

strata and all died at the same time in the Flood. The Carbon 14 date testing procedure dates live hardwood trees at 10,000 years old, live clams at 3,000 years of age, and lava flows, not 200 years old, at three billion years old. As Shakespeare said, "something rotten in the state of Denmark," that is, it is terrible wrong.

16. Prophecies of many earthquakes are being fulfilled, Jews are returning to Israel–as predicted–the Common Market prediction has come true, and many more prophecies have been fulfilled.

17. Three incorrigible criminals have become trustworthy following their conversion to Christ, which gave them a complete change of heart and made them useful citizens. This should happen to everyone to make it a perfect world.

18. There are no missing links of evolution. All species are just as God created them.

19. Prayer, if one uses it, definitely works.

20. Stop sin in the thought stage.

21. You cannot fool, compromise, or tempt God.

22. Heaven's real and much better than the best here.

23. Hell is real, and much worse than the worst here.

24. Never get even. Loving forgiveness is stronger.

25. The smallest living cell is much too complicated to have evolved just by chance.

26. God's plan always and in all ways works, so get acquainted with the author.

A Plea

Thoughts just listed are only a few of the many more infallible evidences in the books I have recommended in the bibliography of resource materials.

Please consult your library or Christian book store, or order the documented helps toward understanding the truth, remembering that it is the truth that makes one free and getting the whole story. Don't take my word for it, but maintain a hungry-for-truth attitude, not biased but wholly honest in your interpretations.

Give God a chance in your life, and His love and all His miraculous wonders will become real and joyous to you as they have for millions of others around the world. Get into His family and in on His inheritance. He is an awesome Father to those who accept Him as Savior and Lord. Don't take a chance on anything other than God's truth.

Talking Sense

Check all I've said in this book for yourself, or are you afraid you will have to face the facts? Many have diligently–and sincerely–tried to disprove the Bible, God, and creation, but found to their amazement that they are really true. Consequently, they accepted Jesus Christ into their heart as Savior and Lord, thereby getting right with God. Like Simon Greenleaf, many have become thoroughly dedicated.

Romans 14:11-12 reads, "'As surely as I live, says the Lord, 'every knee will bow before me; every tongue will confess to God.'" Paul here is quoting from Isaiah 45:23. So why not bow before God now as an accepted child of God, rather than be forced to do it later as a condemned follower of Satan? You will have to do it anyway some day, whether you like it or not.

The apostle Paul says, "Therefore, I urge you, brothers, in view of God's mercy, to offer your bodies as living sacrifices, holy and pleasing to God–this is your spiritual act of worship" (Romans 12:1). Does this make sense to you?

What Kind of God is God?

The triune God cannot run a universe with people in heaven He cannot trust. God could use every one of the six billion people of the world if He could trust each one. This applies to keeping the moral character of the universe pure.

Jehovah is totally a just, pure, and holy God, who knows all aspects of each and every sin committed. He also knows that sin has to be paid for. Prisoners understand this very well as they pay in years or even to the point of execution for their sin. Yet our awesome, great, triune God of the universe–in His matchless love and compassion–desperately does not want anyone to go to

WE CAN DO IT! PAGE 217

hell. He knows perfectly well that when we truly love Him to the extent of accepting Him with our whole heart, He can count on us to do His will.

In order to solve the problem, God sent His one and only Son, who voluntarily left heaven and all its glory and beauty to suffer the ultimate in our place to pay the penalty for our sin debt. Because of His great love for us, Jesus made the sacrifice gladly. His attitude is illustrated by the little boy carrying another boy on his back. He was asked, "Isn't that boy too heavy for you to be carrying? His reply was, "Oh, no! he's my brother."

Another likeness to what Jesus did for us is a father taking the blame for his child's crime and serving his time. Such love would be astonishing.

But does not God and the Godhead do the difficult for us because they love us! Therefore, wasn't it hard for:

1. The Son of God to become the son of man?

2. Jehovah to become Jesus?

3. The King of Kings to leave awesomely beautiful heaven for the wicked filth of earth?

4. The one called Emmanuel to be called a Nazarene? (According to Luke 4:14-28 and John 1:46, Nazareth did not have a good name. We're told from history that the Nazarenes spoke a rude dialect and many were not religious. The Luke passage listed tells of Jesus telling the truth in a

synagogue at Nazareth, which stirred an effort to take his life. The John reference pertains to the question of Nathanael when Philip told him they had found the promised Messiah, Jesus of Nazareth. Nathanael replied, "Nazareth! Can anything good come from there?")

5. The Alpha and Omega, who spoke worlds into existence, to learn to be a carpenter?

6. The creator of the universe to have nowhere to lay His head?

7. The Savior to become a servant?

8. The Bright and Morning Star, the Light of the World, to live in a world of darkness?

9. The sinless Lamb of God to be tempted in all points as we are?

10. The all wise Counselor to be called a lunatic?

11. God, who will some day wipe away all tears from our eyes, to shed tears at a funeral?

12. The Bread of Life to ask a lad for his lunch?

13. The Almighty God to remain silent when blasphemed by His enemies?

14. The Prince of Peace to endure the wrath and beatings of man?

15. The Living Water to say, "I thirst"?

16. The Rose of Sharon to have a crown of thorns crushed into His head?

17. The Resurrection and the Life, the Everlasting One, to be laid in a tomb?

But why did Jesus do all of this for mankind? For the joy set before Him. For you! For me! We sing "Joy to the World," but there are many who do not know and love Him–the One whose birth we celebrate at Christmas. Don't forget Him!

A Final Word

If I have made mistakes, misquoted, or overstated any data in this book, please forgive me and apprise me of my error with solid evidence, not hearsay theories. This is how I see all that I have discussed in this work, and from what I know, I believe it to be fact and not fiction. May God bless you.

Gordon W. Peterson

BIBLIOGRAPHY

Baugh, Carl E., *Creation in Symphony,* video-taped lecture, 3 vols., Creation Evidence Museum, P.O. Box 205, Glen Rose, TX 76043.

Bright, William (Bill) R., *The Four Spiritual Laws* (with a worldwide distribution in excess of 2.5 billion). Available 50 @ $8.99. Bright is also founder of Campus Crusade for Christ, which shows *The Jesus Film* worldwide. New Life Publications, P.O. Box 593684, Orlando, FL 32859-3684.

Criswell, W.A., *Why I Preach that the Bible Is Literally True*, Broadman Press, Nashville, TN.

Crouch, Paul, Trinity Broadcasting Network (700+ TV stations, 12 satellites, short-and long-wave radio, and over 4,500 cable stations). P.O. Box A, Santa Ana, CA. 92711-2101

D'Armond, David, *Evidence Against Evolution & Evidence for Creation* tapes, Institute for Creation Research and Museum (many informative books on creation), P.O. Box 2667, El Cajon, CA 92021.

Eastman, Dick, Every Home for Christ, president, P.O. Box 35930, Colorado Springs, CO 80935. Their goal is to witness to every home in the world by year 2,000.

Glass, Bill, ministries of Champions for Today (youth organization), citywide evangelistic crusades, & prison ministry. P.O. Box 9000, Cedar Hill, TX 75106-2349. Among Glass's books are *Expect To Win*, Word Books, Waco, TX, 1984, 3rd printing & *How To Win When the*

Roof CaVes In, Fleming H. Revell, Old Tappan, New Jersey, 1988.

Graham, Billy, Billy Graham Evangelistic Association, worldwide evangelist & prolific author. P.O. Box 779, Minneapolis, MN 55440-0779.

Jeffery, Grant, *Signature of God*, Frontier Research Publications, P.O. Box 47070, Tulsa, OK 74147-0470.

Johnson, Philip E., *Darwin on Trial*, InterVarsity Press, Downers Grove, IL 60515. Johnson, a graduate of Harvard and Chicago U., taught law at the University of California, Berkeley, CA.

Kennedy, D. James, *Evangelism Explosion, Why I Believe, What If the Bible Had Never Been Written*, Coral Ridge Ministries, P.O. Box 40, Ft. Lauderdale, FL 33302-0040.

LaLonde, Peter & Paul, hosts of TV program, *This Week in Bible Prophecy*; authors of *301 Startling Proofs & Prophecies* (proving that God exists). Prophecy Partners, Inc., P.O. Box 665, Niagara Falls, Ontario, L2E 6V5.

Malz, Betty, *My Glimpses of Eternity* (book & tape), M&M Communications, P.O. Box 564, Crystal Beach, FL 34681.

McCoy, Mike, national director, Champions for Today, 551 Exam Court, Lawrenceville, GA 30244. Available for bookings in school, church, and youth groups.

McDowell, Josh, *Evidence That Demands a Verdict,* 2 vols., *Answers to Tough Questions,* Thomas Nelson Publishers, P.O. Box 141000, Nashville, TN 37214-1000.

Morris, Henry M., *Many Infallible Proofs* and *The Modern Creation Trilogy,* 3 vols., Institute for Creation Research P.O. Box 2667, El Cajon, CA 92021. Several of Dr. Morris's books have been written with sons and grandsons. Dr. Morris is an authority on science and creation at the institute.

Murphy ("Murf the Surf"), Jack Roland, *Jewels for the Journey,* publisher Chaplain Ray, International Prison Ministry, P.O. Box 63, Dallas, TX 75221. Murphy was given two life sentences, plus 20 years in prison for jewelry theft. While *in stir,* he was saved and changed by the Lord Jesus Christ and has become a trustworthy citizen. A popular and dynamic speaker, he is heard around the world.

Myers, John, *Voices from the Edge of Eternity,* Spire Books, Old Tappan, New Jersey 07675. The book covers some 250 out-of-body experiences (to heaven and hell) from the Roman Emperor Nero's mother (Agrippina II, A.D. 16? to 59?) to 1968.

Rawlings, Maurice S., M.D., *Beyond Death's Door, To Hell and Back, Death Strand,* Thomas Nelson Publishers, Nashville, TN. Death is described as it happened. Dr. Rawlings is a specialist in cardiovascular diseases in hospitals of Chattanooga, Tennessee, and professor of medicine for the University of Tennessee.

224 BIBLIOGRAPHY

Ross, Hugh, *Scientific Proof That God Is.* Dr. Ross is an astronomy professor. No address available. Check with your Bible book store.

Salem, Cheryl, and family, *A Bright Shining Place* and a tape, *The Music and the Ministry of Cheryl Prewitt Salem.* Cheryl Salem Ministries, P. O. Box 701287, Tulsa, OK 74170. Cheryl is Miss America 1980.

Sekulow, Jay A., The American Center for Law & Justice, P.O. Box 450349, Atlanta, GA 31145-0349.

Slocum, Marianna, *The Good Seed,* Promise Publishing Co., Orange, CA 92668. Slocum completed Bible translations and a dialect in two different languages while with Wycliffe Bible Translators. Three hundred plus churches were established in Chiapas, Mexico, from one translation and a dialect.

Tyndale House Publishers, Inc., *The One Year Bible*, a guide that carries the reader through the Bible in one year. See page 186 for the plan's details.

Wycliffe Bible Translators, P.O. Box 2727, Huntington Beach, CA 92647. WBT needs translators, literacy workers, and professional support workers. WBT is an important and worthy mission, meriting your support.

INDEX

AIDS, 27, 69
  See also venereal diseases
Alaska, trip to, 52, 53
Alcatraz, 99
Alpha and Omega, 218
apple, one rotten, 89
automobile prophecy of, 31, 32
  servicing and upkeep, 87

Baptist, John the, 168
Barabbus, 170
behemoth, 39
Bethlehem, 167
betting, 13-16
  and athletic events, 13, 14
  and casino gambling, 14
  and fortune-telling, 15
  and horse racing, 14
  and lottery, 14
  and political elections, 13
  and sweepstakes, 14, 15
Bible, 127
  printing of, 201, 202
  reading plan for, 186
  translating, 127-133
  what it contains, 209
big bang theory, 33
Billy Graham ministry, 28, 207
Brabon, J., 103-108
Bright, Bill, 192
Bundy, Ted, 86

Calling by God, 180, 181
Campus Crusade for Christ, 28, 29, 182
carbon fourteen theory, 37

Carter, Jimmy, 57
Cephus (Peter), 78, 111
Chaffin, Bill, 116
Champions for Today, 117
Chicago, Cook County Jail, 118, 119
children of God, 179
Christianity unlawful, 27
church in Dallas, 155
  why join one, 191
churches
  quitting God, 73
  supporting hate groups, 90
  what kind is yours?, 110
Clark, Anthony, 116
Colombia, nation of, 103
  Bella Vista Prison, 103
  Medellin, 103
Columbia, space shuttle, 70
conscience salved, 95
Cook County Jail, 118, 119
counterfeits, 201
creation
  beauty of, 93
  evidence of, 36
  scientists from El Cajon, CA or Glen Rose, TX, 207
Cummings, David, 208

Darrow, Clarence, 37, 176
Darwin, Charles, 176, 195
dinosaurs, 39-41
dog stories, 177, 178

Egypt, 167
Eisenhower, Dwight D., 176

El Cajon, CA, scientists, 207
European Common Market, 32
Evangelism Explosion, 29
evolution, 198, 207

fasting, 163
Fatow, Sandi, 100-102
fishers of men, 187
first and greatest commandment, 157
forgiveness, 91, 92, 124, 127, 190-191
fossils, 36, 41
Four Spiritual Laws, 193
foxholes, 36, 41
Franklin, Benjamin, 67-68

Gerdel, Florence, 128-130
Glass, Bill, 117
Glass, Bill, Prison Ministry, 113, 114-116, 118, 208
Glen Rose, TX, scientists, 207
God calls us personally, 180-181
gods, 71
Gold Book, little, 192
good persona, 84
Graham, Billy
  first sermon, 109
  ministry of, 28, 207
gravity, God's law of, 41, 84, 165
Great Commission, 92, 187
Greenleaf, Simon, 175, 176
Harvey, 57, 59

hate, 87, 90
haunted houses, 71
healing miracles, 43-49
  Baxter, Ms., 45
  Dakota church, 44
  Maltz, Betty, 45-49
  Salem, Cheryl, 43, 44
heavenly existence, 52, 94
hell, 154
Herod, King, 167
Hitler, Adolf, 59
Holt, Don, 99-100, 114

Ifugao area Philippines, 131
"I've always been a Christian," 156

Jeffery, Grant, 26
Jerusalem, 167
Jesus Christ
  and awesome love of, 211
  baptism of, 168
  betrayal of, 73
  crucifixion of, 75, 77, 170
  and feeding the multitudes, 23, 81, 82, 110
  first advent of, 24, 25
  and Model Prayer, 150
  mystique of, 75, 76
  and plain talk to disciples, 146
  and prayers for: all believers, Himself, His disciples, 147, 148
  rising of, 170, 171, 174
  second advent of, 26, 27, 30
  and suffering for us, 174
  and His temple visit, 167

Jesus (continued)
  and tempted by Satan, 168
  and warning of false
    Christs, 26, 28
  washing disciples' feet,
    77, 78, 144
Joshua, 22, 23
Judas Iscariot, 169

Kinnaman, J. O., 183
Kennedy, D. James, 208

leviathan, 40

magnetism of earth, 35, 36
Maltz, Betty, 45-49
"mark of the beast," 29, 30
Mary, mother of Jesus, 210
McCoy, Mike, 117
Mexico, Chiapas, 128-130
miracles, see healing
  miracles
Moody D. Lyman, 109
Moses, 16-20, 21-22
"Mother Nature," 38
Murphy, Jack, 99, 100, 102,
  114, 200
National Day of Prayer, 152
national debt, 63, 205, 206
Nazareth, 167
"Nebraska man," 37
Noah
  and ark, 33
  and flood, 40-42

"One Year Bible" reading
  plan, 186
Orlando, 105, 108

Oscar, 103-108, 112. (Oscar
and Orlando are converted
Christians from Bella Vista
Prison in Medellin,
Colombia.)
out-of-body experiences, 49-
  51, 53-56

Paul, the apostle, 32, 82,
  216
persecution is to be
  expected, 74
Peter
  Cephas, 111
  Simon, 78
Peterson, Eric and Carol,
  137, 138
Peterson, Gordon
  conversion, 177
  fall, breaking wrist and
    hip, 135-137
Pharisees, 169
Pilate, Pontius, 170
prayer by Jesus
  prays all night, 138
  prays on cross for His
    enemies, 142
  prays in Gethsemane, 141,
    142
  prays high priestly prayer,
    143
  See also Jesus Christ
    and prayer for:
prayer
  admonishment for, 185
  by kidnaped girl, 143
  National Day of, 152
  pattern of, 152-154

prayer (continued)
  prayer, 24 hour vigils, 202
  prayer, World Day of, 152
prisons, 82, 99, 103
prison warden, 113
promiscuous living, 63
Promise Keepers, 208
Psalms, 154

Rawlings, Maurice S., 54-55
revivals
  urgent need of, 200
  planning for, 206, 207-209
Rudman, Dick, 136-137
Russia, 140

Salem, Cheryl, 43-44
salvation
  explanation of, 183, 184
  key to, 165, 179, 180
  prayer for, 182
Satan, 160, 165
Schweitzer, Albert, 83
Scopes trial, 37
scribes, 169
Slocum, Marianna, 128
society, degradation of, 197
soldiers, Roman, 170
Sweden, 89

Trinity Broadcasting Network, 28
teen-age violence, 200, 201
Thompson, Harold, 99, 100, 114
tithes, the 121-123

Titus, 83
translators, 28, 127-132, 202
trend, the downward plunge of, 99
truth, importance of, 89
Tzeltal Indians, 128-130

venereal diseases, 70
See also AIDS

Washington, D.C.
  measurement gauges in, 62
  prayer vigils in, 206
Wycliffe Bible Translators, 28, 127-132, 208
World Day of Prayer, 152

"Ye must be born again," 180